Dynamic Strategies
for Small Business

Dynamic Strategies for Small Business

Sviatoslav Steve Seteroff, DBA
and
Lydia Guadalupe Campuzano, DBA

Dynamic Strategies for Small Business

First published in 2010 by
Business Expert Press, LLC
222 East 46th Street, New York, NY 10017
www.businessexpertpress.com

ISBN-13: 978-160649-153-9 (paperback)

ISBN-13: 978-160649-154-6 (e-book)

DOI 10.4128/9781606491546

A publication in the Business Expert Press Strategic Management collection

Collection ISSN: 2150-9611 (print)
Collection ISSN: 2150-9646 (electronic)

Cover design by Jonathan Pennell
Interior design by Scribe, Inc.

First edition: September 2010

10 9 8 7 6 5 4 3 2 1

Printed in Taiwan

This book is lovingly dedicated to Leanne DeBroeck, who has blessed us unconditionally with her thoughtfulness and time.

All Good Things Come in Threes . . .

Photo by Lydia Campuzano 2010
Inspired by my coauthor Steve Seteroff

Please visit us on the web
www.strategicspirituality.org

Abstract

Formulation of a strategic plan for small business can be an envigorating experience for the small business owner. The potential for reducing costs, and time consuming practices, can be eliminated by implementing this innovative dynamic strategies model. The tools of analysis are straight forward and can be applied by any individual. This book will assist you in developing a viable strategic plan for your business that will be brief, clear, concise, and easily understood. The benefits of the dynamic strategies model may increase commitment to excellence, effectiveness of performance, and profits. An innovative approach to empowering the employees of an organization is presented. This dynamic approach assists in building a holistic organizational culture that fosters commitment across all levels of the organization. This book is a blend of traditional techniques with a new perspective of strategy. It is important to remember that it is people that make the difference, and we must never forget that although we manage things, we must lead people.

Keywords

Strategy, Business, Spirituality, Planning, Profitability, Management, Leadership, Motivation, Satisfaction, Empowerment, Diversity, Organizations, Culture, Vision, Mission, Goals, Objectives

Contents

Introduction

We welcome you to explore the wonderful world of strategic planning at a level that is appropriate to a business of whatever size and market but that is especially tailored to address the small business and entrepreneur. Students in an MBA or DBA program at most universities culminate their studies with a capstone course in which all the elements of the program are brought into play in order to conduct analyses and to develop the course product, a strategic business plan.[1] Yes, it is clear that two or more years of coursework are essential for effectively performing the analyses at the academic level. It is also clear that the one who knows the business best is the individual who is deeply entrenched in the day-to-day operations. For the busy small-business owner, the time available for study at the academic level is limited, and it detracts from the ability of the organization to remain both viable and competitive.

Our objective is not to detract from the tried and proven approaches to strategic planning that have served so well for so many years—ranging from Bennis,[2] Byars,[3] Hill,[4] Landrum,[5] and others—across so many varied organizations. Our objective is to recognize the small-business owner, the entrepreneur, and the employee of a small organization. They know deep in their being that the only way for the business to survive is to be flexible and to meet the demands of the customer right now and in such a way as to not squander the resources of the firm. These individuals know the product, the available resources, the customers, and what it takes to succeed. How can we fail to recognize this knowledge?

Because there are few barriers between the employee and the owner, who is deeply involved in all aspects of the business, it is an ideal way to recognize the internal knowledge that is available to draw upon. Where larger organizations struggle with how to empower their employees,[6] employees in a small business are critically aware that their continued employment depends on their performance in making the organization successful. Where larger organizations are concerned with titles, the small business owner will pitch in to accomplish the most mundane chores to ensure that business objectives are met. Granted that although the majority of business in the United States is small or entrepreneurial, we continue to address the needs of larger organizations, often to the exclusion of these small employers who are responsible for the bulk of the employment.

Steve Martin, responding to a question regarding the percentage of jobs in the United States attributed to small business, responds, in part,

> Small businesses (defined as having fewer than 500 employees) represent a major part of the economy and account for 50% of employment in the United States, and according to the U.S. Small Business Administration, create 60 to 80% of new jobs. The U.S. Bureau of the Census reports that of 113.4 million non-farm private sector workers in 2003, small firms with fewer than 500 workers employed 57.4 million (50.6%). Firms with fewer than 100 employees employed 41.0 million (36%).[7]

As we look carefully at small business, we see that the culture is vastly different from what we expect to find in the large and well-established organizations. The United States Small Business Administration (SBA) is clear that most small business fails because of a lack of capital and lack of planning. Lenders and banks issuing lines of credit are insistent on the small business owner having a business plan,[8] and they will often guarantee the line of credit with an attachment on the real property of the small business owner rather the business for which the business plan was prepared. One wonders, then, how much value the business plan has if the line of credit is not based on the plan but on the market value of the owner's home. In any case, the purpose here is not to investigate the banking industry but to determine the strategy that a business must develop before a viable business plan can be created.

We look at the development of the strategic plan in plain business language, using project management tools to ensure clarity and a systematic approach. We also take into consideration the cultural aspects at play in any organization, especially the small business organization, regardless of where it may be located or the customer base it has. We invite you to join us in our investigation of several issues involved in the creation of a strategic plan that is flexible and adaptable. The plan must serve the needs of the individuals of a small business organization as it functions in a day-to-day operating environment and grows to maturity.

We believe the approach is scalable and, although our experience has been with small business, the process should not change as the organization grows. We have added the enterprise-level component to accommodate several strategic business units. As more resources become available, it is entirely feasible to apply them toward the use of more traditional tools of analysis in order to refine the approach of developing the plan. As the organization continues to be empowered to act as needed, the implementation should not be affected. We invite your implementation comments.

CHAPTER 1

Makings of an Organization

From earliest history, humans have gathered in groups—which could be considered early forms of organizations—for protection, mutual support, and sharing expertise in accomplishing complex tasks. In the earliest days, clan organization was common because, as a species, humans learned from pack animals that hunting and protection of one's kin were both more effective in groups. The clan was usually headed by a leader who coordinated the activities of the members in hunting, fishing, salt mining, gathering, cooking, healing, spiritual needs, and protection, among other areas specific to survival. As prosperity led to a surplus of goods, and as adjacent clans learned of the excess productivity, trade developed, and an economy was created that ranged from an exchange of goods, or a barter system, to some form of accounting using coinage or another medium of exchange. As societies developed, and as societal structures became more complex, a hierarchical approach to leadership developed. This approach was effective through two industrial revolutions. A worldwide economy continued to mature and reinvent itself as needs were identified. Changes in the operating environment were recognized as opportunities, and a realization emerged that existing corporate control systems were not meeting the needs of the organization.[1] Today, our traditional organizations are largely hybrids. Hybrid organizations incorporate a hierarchical structure, with some elements of a matrix organizational structure in order to conserve human resources. Hybrid organizations often incorporate the strengths of the clan leadership organizational structure as informal organizations.[2] As society has learned that flexibility is key to the survival of public and private entities, organizational structures have continued to mature.

Traditional Organizations

Traditional organizations have evolved from hierarchical organizations based on a top-down flow of information. The premise is that knowledge comes from above, and subordinates learn from superiors. Innovation is not generally encouraged. Innovation is rewarded when, in extremis, an employee is forced out of established and approved processes, and the result is favorable to the organization. Leaders are taught to inspire their subordinates, and subordinates are taught to obey their superiors. The organization favors conformance and encourages stability, while discouraging risk taking. In such a traditional organization, employees are encouraged to follow complex and well-documented processes and discouraged from modifying the established rules without seeking permission from supervisors. The supervisors, in turn, are encouraged to enforce the rules and processes and discouraged from innovative thoughts. Work rules are enforced. Active participation by the employees in complying with the plan or process is the objective of the leadership. A system of rewards and punishments is in place to ensure that the desirable characteristics are encouraged.

Empowered Organizations

An empowered organization is one in which employees are permitted to make decisions supported by organizational leaders. Risk taking is at least tolerated, and often encouraged, especially among trusted employees. A system of rewards is generally emphasized, and punishment is minimized. The concentration is on rewarding excellence in performance through recognition, promotion, and bonus systems. Employees are actively encouraged to develop themselves personally through outside education with social activities and internally through formal and informal training. Employees are encouraged to offer suggestions and scan the external environment for opportunities for the organization and for changes that may threaten operations. Suggestions and information from employees are valued, and leaders pay close attention to the employees. In an empowered organization, employees are valued and leaders expend considerable resources to ensure the most appropriate mix of employees is developed into a culture of commitment to the organization.

Most small business organizations fall into the category of empowered organizations. Small business organizations must leverage several qualifications of each employee to make use of the knowledge across several disciplines. Each employee is recognized for the contribution they make toward a successful outcome for the organization. The leader of the organization dismisses the advice and suggestions of an employee at the peril of reducing the already slim margin of success that a small business organization enjoys. Most small business owners or leaders place great value and trust in their employees. Granted, new employees may need some time to become accepted, but once accepted, they enjoy a level of trust that is seldom seen in larger organizations outside the executive level. Small business employees often make decisions reserved for vice presidents in larger organizations, and they enjoy the support and confidence of their leaders in daily operations that is seldom seen in larger organizations.

Some small business organizations grow rapidly, and they quickly begin to rely on full-time professional managers. Some small business organizations prefer to remain small and purposefully limit, or halt, growth. Most small business organizations expand slowly and carefully, taking the advice of their existing employees in the hiring process. When existing employees are consulted about expansion, they will frequently recommend like-minded individuals who will quickly fit into the existing organizational culture. When expansion includes employees in the planning process, a spiritual business organization begins to emerge.

Spiritual Business Organizations

It is important to make a distinction between a spiritual business organization and a spiritual workplace. A spiritual workplace is based on finding meaning and purpose at work. A spiritual business organization includes the characteristics of both a traditional and an empowered organization, and it encompasses a culture that promotes the human potential of the empowered employees.

In formulating a definition of the "spiritual" business organization, there are some topics that should first be addressed. First, the word spirituality is a term that is easily misunderstood, and the term often makes people nervous. Second, misconceptions of the meaning of spirituality come from the broad range of definitions available for this term. The term "spirituality" encompasses various meanings that typically vary by context and by author. Finally, "spirituality," a "spiritual" workplace, and other similar terms have not been formalized with a consensus within academia or in the business world.

The attack on the World Trade Center on September 11, 2001, established a benchmark for advocating for a spiritual workplace.[3] Developing a spiritual workplace includes finding a deeper meaning and a sincere purpose.[4] A spiritual business organization embraces a more complete culture beyond that of an empowered organization, including tolerance, acceptance, and embracing the beliefs of others.

The following paragraphs will delve further into the several steps toward establishing the components of a spiritual business organization (see Figure 1.1). The sections will specifically address the progression through *tolerance* of diversity, progress to *inclusion* by diversity, and culminate with *embracing* diversity. Later in this book, we will point out that as an organization establishes spirituality, productivity is enhanced, voluntary employee turnover is reduced, and profitability is increased.

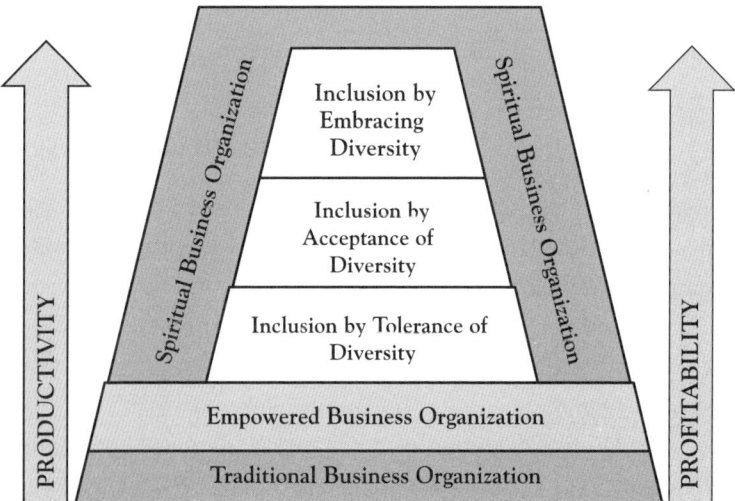

Figure 1.1. Progression to a spiritual business organization (© 2010 Campuzano & Seteroff).

Inclusion by Tolerance of Diversity

The initial step in attaining a spiritual business organization occurs when the employees gain a level of tolerance for diversity of other employees within the workplace. Employees in an empowered organization begin to transition toward a spiritual business organization when other employees begin to tolerate the deep-rooted beliefs of coworkers. The objective is to tolerate differences on the job beyond the human resource requirements. The culture of the organization changes to one of tolerance for diversity and concentrates on the accomplishment of organizational objectives. As tolerance spreads in the organization, cliques remain, but exclusivity is no longer as pronounced. Mutual respect takes on a more readily apparent role. Trust in each other to perform well in a cooperative environment becomes culturally entrenched. Morality tends to manifest itself within a safer environment, which begins to reduce tensions and involvement of leaders in mitigating disputes. Employees become more aware of the differences of their peers and tolerate beliefs other than their own.

Inclusion by Acceptance of Diversity

Moving beyond tolerance to acceptance manifests itself as employees begin to look for similarities in their beliefs and to avoid concentrating on the differences. As acceptance begins to permeate an organization, a greater concentration on similarities appears in the organizational culture. The employees become increasingly aware of the capabilities each possesses, and they are able to leverage their strengths to accomplish organizational objectives in a more economical manner. Mutual respect becomes an accepted practice, with a deeper understanding and acceptance of diversity. Trust increases and may expand outside the work environment. Morality takes hold, and employees create a safe working environment that begins to expand beyond the workplace, with a greater responsibility for each other's welfare. Differences are still in place, but the concentration is on the similarities in individual beliefs and the mutual effort is focused on accomplishing the objectives of the organization.

Inclusion by Embracing Diversity

Embracing cultural diversity is probably rare in a secular environment because of equal opportunity requirements, but it is theoretically possible for employees who can move beyond acceptance in the workplace. When beliefs are relatively homogenous, embracing diversity becomes possible. The transition becomes possible when employees understand both the differences in tolerance and the similarities in acceptance. The next quantum step is embracing similarities and creating a new culture based on mutual respect, trust, and morality. Such activity can elevate the organizational culture to a potential that creates a safe and productive working environment. When employees embrace diversity, this attitude spreads through the work environment and also transcends artificial boundaries, creating an extended family that incorporates the diversity of the employees. At this point, work becomes almost like play. Work is fun, and employees produce at optimum levels with little need for direction because the organization has arrived at a point where all employees are aware of its objectives. Each employee is dedicated to achieving the greatest success possible as individuals, collectively, and for the good of the organization. Leaders emerge as necessary, and leaders become followers by voluntarily subordinating themselves for the good of the task, the mission, or the organization.[1]

Summary

A spiritual business organization does not include religious dogma, the proselytizing, or the evangelizing of one's religion to convert another employee. Religions such as Christianity, Islam, Buddhism, and other dogma may influence a spiritual business organization, but the intention of a spiritual business organization is not to provide a free forum to convert other employees into any religious sect. The purpose of a spiritual business organization is to empower the employee, promote human potential, and establish a spiritual ambiance. A spiritual ambiance includes the values of respect, integrity, and honesty. Beyond these values is the notion of performing at a level of excellence because there is a belief in a higher power, a deity, or God. Now this is where the issues arise, as the Christian God is viewed by Christians as being different from the Islamic God, as viewed by Muslims, and so forth with other religions and dogmatic practices. The idea is to embrace one's own personal God and perform to one's highest potential. Again, the spiritual business organization supports the notion that the organization will be operated by the leaders with integrity, respect, and honesty. To be a spiritual business organization implies that the leadership will move the organizational culture beyond tolerance to a point where there is acceptance of each employee despite the different beliefs in a higher power, a deity, or God.

The spiritual business organization encompasses spirituality and total acceptance. A spiritual business organization does not support a specific religious dogma or religious rite. Simply stated, a spiritual business organization provides an environment where employees are empowered; the values of trust, integrity, honesty, and respect are upheld; and there is acceptance of the religious beliefs of others. This concept might be contrary to many religious beliefs, but when one examines the Christian and Buddhist concepts—as well as other concepts such as "love one another"—the spiritual business organization is empowered.

CHAPTER 2

Beyond a Costly Strategic Business Model

Strategic business models used in generating strategic business plans in industry today are very detailed, lengthy, and elaborate.[1] The problem is that in most cases, no one reads these strategic business plans. Much credence is placed in every employee knowing the vision or mission statement. That is certainly an advantage, and many organizations go to extraordinary means to display the statements prominently. In at least two examples from personal experience, companies printed and distributed laminated cards containing the vision and mission statements for each employee to carry with their employee identification badge. Working as consultants, we were exposed to one such organization, and the executive in charge of the initiative was very proud that every employee had quick access to the mission statement in this particular case.[2] Unfortunately, very few understood the statement, and even fewer understood how to comply with the statement when faced with a situation that required deviation from the routine instructions.

The Challenge for Organizational Leaders Is Communication

Leaders may be able to formulate a vision statement, formulate a mission statement, and even establish goals for their organizations, but unless these can be communicated effectively across all levels of the organization, the effort becomes very limited in implementation. Our experience leads us to believe that most plans are too complex, too detailed, and too lengthy to be clear at the implementation level. How then should we structure our communications? We need to instill a clear understanding of the desired business direction into the minds and hearts of our employees so that they can individually make tactical decisions when issues not covered by routine guidance arise.

Procedures are largely a managerial issue, and we are generally very good at providing guidance for routine operations. Today, in a fast-paced, often global, operating environment, flexibility is required. We are also faced with emergent changes being driven from within and without the organization. Employees at all levels of the organization may be required to act independently to either mitigate potential challenges or to take advantage of opportunities that arise unexpectedly. Leaders must communicate a clear understanding of the parameters of the decision-making authority and the desired business direction. Knowing the desired direction can greatly assist in ensuring that, when faced with an opportunity, an empowered employee makes a correct decision that will further the organizational objectives at the tactical level. Keeping communications brief, clear, and concise makes the task of meeting the organizational objectives easier.

Genesis: Edward Pierce (1996)

We must begin this work with an acknowledgement of a pioneer, Dr. Edward Pierce, in his attempt to make the strategic planning process understandable to doctoral students from around the world and to make the process simpler and affordable across a wide range of business entities. In 1995 and 1996, Dr. Pierce introduced his doctoral students at Nova Southeastern University to a bare-bones model that made the strategic planning process clear without detracting from the myriad components that make up a strategic plan in the true sense. His dedication to making the complex simple, while recognizing the underlying complexity in the traditional linear approach, allowed many of his students, and the companies he consulted with, to understand the reason behind the process.

Edward Pierce is now retired, but his legacy lives on through several iterations and through many implementations across diverse organizations on at least three continents. As presented, the strategic business model began with the clean and clear definitions Pierce envisioned. The model has changed dramatically as successive implementations drove a need to add business language, a project management approach, and the clarity to ensure that a small business owner, or entrepreneur, could grasp the concepts and implement the underlying principles without resorting to the traditional high-cost linear approach. As the Dynamic Strategies Model currently stands, it bears only superficial relation to the model presented by Pierce, but the clarity and simplicity remain.

Why the Need for a Dynamic Strategies Model?

The dynamic strategic model is more flexible and easier to understand than traditional linear models. The traditional linear approach, with the built-in iterations, is versatile during the development stages but lacks flexibility at the tactical level. It is also costly to develop because it consumes resources that small businesses simply do not have or are unwilling to commit funding to. A lender seldom requires a strategic plan, so small business owners often skip this preliminary step and proceed to the business plan without the clear direction that a strategic planning process contributes. When educated owners of small business, or entrepreneurs, understand the value of a strategic plan, they generally attempt to apply the linear process learned in their graduate programs. This reliance on the robust linear approach tends to perpetuate the complexity and lack of flexibility that the traditional approach entails. Business, especially at the small-business level, requires the flexibility to respond quickly and appropriately to emerging changes in the operating environment so that a clear understanding of the direction is essential. An additional benefit of the Dynamic Strategies Model is that it allows the development of a viable plan at a comparatively low cost.

High Cost of Traditional Plans

Traditional plans are driven from the top down, and larger organizations will devote a considerable amount of time and effort applying as many of the tools of analysis as possible to ensure a robust and comprehensive strategic plan. Larger organizations will have a unit dedicated to the development of a strategic plan. The strategic planning unit will often remain in place to monitor and adjust the plan throughout the year. More often, the update is an annual event with considerable effort in implementing the guidance from senior leaders. The top-down method is a typical approach to using the robust traditional linear model. The linear approach has stood the test of time, and the double looping to ensure compliance and alignment becomes an excellent approach.

Perhaps a brief explanation of looping is in order at this point. In a single loop, we implement, evaluate, and formulate a change and then apply it to whatever the process may be. In double looping, we would continue to evaluate and adjust as necessary after each change in the process (see Figure 2.1). This double loop process is robust and has become a part of the strategic planning process. For organizations that are able to use internal resources to develop and monitor a strategic plan, the benefits are manifold. Even for medium-sized firms that invest in the development and annual update of a strategic plan using outside resources, the benefits can be substantial. In both cases, the benefits lie mainly in the development process, as once the strategic plan is developed, it is seldom consulted. The benefits of the plan are derived from the policies that are developed from the plan or modified as a result of an update to the plan. The plan itself remains static between revisions.

In a typical linear approach, as in the dynamic model, the chief executive officer or business owner must establish the long-term direction for the organization. The difference between the two models is that in the dynamic model, the small business owner must not only consider but must also ensure alignment with the culture of the organization. Setting the objectives is typically the responsibility of the executive level, and this does not change for the dynamic model, except that in a small business, contributions to the strategic and business plans would be sought from all levels of the organization. In larger organizations, this would not be feasible. In the traditional linear model, determining, or designing, the strategy is in

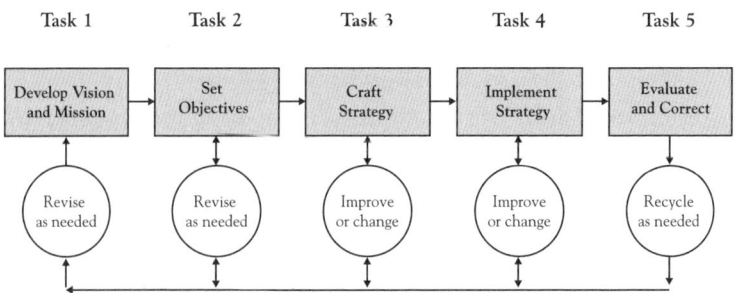

Figure 2.1. A typical strategic planning process flow chart (adapted from various sources).

the domain of the organizational leaders, and the management has responsibility for the implementation and evaluation of the performance.

The traditional models are very robust in that they are sequential, with each node contributing to the strength of the whole and a well-established feedback loop. For example, if the objectives do not align with the vision and mission statements, the statements are changed or the objectives are revised until consonance is achieved. The same holds true for designing the strategy, and the comparison is then to vision statements and previous tasks, objectives, and the mission. Each step in the linear process is compared to the preceding step for alignment, and also to every previous step, until consonance is achieved (see Figure 2.1). This constant looping creates a robust strategic plan. The same process continues for the rest of the linear process. Here is where the dynamic model we propose differs—this approach drives the process to the lowest possible level of the organization, allowing movement toward a relationship approach. The relationship approach allows for changing only the elements of the plan that are affected by an emergent change, without having to progress through the model in a specific manner.

Better Use of Small Business Resources

Small businesses, even those whose principals have the benefit of a graduate education and are aware of strategic planning, often forego development of a strategic plan for several reasons. The main reason is that they are too busy staying competitive to allocate resources to the creation of a strategic plan. Additionally, lenders concentrate on a business plan rather than a strategic plan, so the emphasis is placed where the lender directs. We quickly forget that in the most basic terms, we must first have a direction—a strategic plan—before we can develop a business plan, but because the United States Small Business Administration (SBA) stresses a business plan,[3] the emphasis is placed on this. In practice, the business plan incorporates the elements of a strategic plan in its formulation and contains many of the attributes needed for a strategic plan.

Unlike the traditional linear strategic plan, the approach of the Dynamic Strategies Model is to distribute the formulation of the plan across all levels of an organization. Depending on the number of employees, and their level of commitment, the approach is flexible enough to use a top-down approach, where the small business owner develops the entire plan. The alternative is a bottom-up approach, where each employee contributes to the process. Another approach is a hybrid, where the best combination approach utilizes available resources to the best advantage. This flexibility, and the attendant brevity, is perhaps the most important benefit of the planning process.

Plan Available at All Organizational Levels

Traditional plans are generally made available to most supervisory levels of the organization, but all levels are usually not consulted on a regular basis because of the sheer size of the document and because its availability is often limited. Employees almost never have access to the strategic plan itself, and when they do have access, it is generally only to the portions of the strategic plan that affect the specific area of employment. The sole exception is that many companies make a sincere effort to ensure all employees at least know, or understand, the vision and mission statements. Because of the voluminous nature of the traditional strategic plan and its limited availability, reliance is generally placed on the policies that are driven by the strategic plan, as these are usually where the metrics are embedded. As Richard Hodgetts[4] stated, "that which gets measured, gets done,"[5] so the policies are consulted instead of the strategic plan itself. This is a limitation of the traditional approach because it lacks flexibility. The Dynamic Strategies Model offers an approach that is brief, clear, concise, and understandable at all levels of the organization, and it offers a working document that can be modified as necessary.

Decisions Are Quicker

Decisions can be made quicker when all employees have access to the same document. When the document is also brief, clear, and concise, the direction is more easily understood. If the direction of the organization is clear, then changes in the operating environment can be recognized, and the approach may be modified as necessary to meet the changing demands of the operational environment. Employees are able to make decisions with greater confidence, and leaders and managers can then concentrate on empowering the employees as a means of increasing organizational commitment and employee satisfaction. A spiritual business organization promotes employees to perform at a level of excellence[6] without fear and within a safe environment and selects leaders who lead by cognition and compassion. There is evidence[7] to support that empowered employees function best in an organization that fosters a spiritual and moral business environment where mutual respect and trust are prevalent. The combination of a dynamic and flexible strategic plan with empowered employees can be a significant competitive advantage for a firm.

Opportunities Are Recognized Earlier

In a spiritual business organization where employees are empowered, and where there is a transition from participation to commitment, opportunities can be recognized earlier because employees are aware of their empowerment to act swiftly to capture first-mover advantage.[8] When individual employees understand the direction of the organization and know their own part within its structure, mutual respect and trust are generated by a spiritualized leader. The spiritualized leader provides the moral approach that adds to the empowerment and confidence of the employee to move forward in the absence of policy or specific guidance. When employees are committed, and when they are encouraged to make decisions in the best interests of the organization, more options become available. The employees may be rewarded for taking appropriate action, and the organization tends to reinforce the positive aspects of the process, which further contributes to mutual respect and trust. The risk lies in the propensity to step outside the area of mutual respect and trust to condemn inappropriate actions rather than using them as learning experiences. Part of the strategic plan must be a commitment to continuous learning and the creation and maintenance of a safe working environment. Part of the process then becomes selecting employees that are committed for retention and promotion, while identifying employees who consistently lack commitment for replacement. Committed employees who are aware of the organizational direction, and who are empowered to act in response to changes in the operating environment, tend to conserve resources.

Resources Are Better Employed

Organizational leaders, managers, and supervisors are overhead and so must constantly strive to improve the effectiveness of the employees entrusted to their areas of responsibility. In an empowered workforce where each employee becomes committed to the success of the organization, sensitivity toward conserving resources becomes paramount. Employees will seek out ways to perform assigned tasks in the least amount of time and will waste fewer physical resources. Frequently, employees who are asked to contribute to the strategies developed by the organization for accomplishing specific tasks identify methods to ease their performance of the task. The empowered employees will take advantage of emergent technology to perform at a more cost-effective level. An example of this was vividly displayed by a mechanic in a second-tier aerospace company who was asked why there were so many failures by a consultant called in to assist after the responsible engineers were unable to identify the cause of the problem.[9] The problem was that the mechanics operating the machine were very aware of the number of failures, but the engineer supervisor allowed them to violate the process instructions to reduce the number of failures. When the process instructions were not followed, the number of failures fell within acceptable limits, and a penciled notation was made on the mechanics copy of the process instructions. However, since neither the supervising engineer nor the mechanic reported this notation, the operative process instructions were not changed. On review, the number of failures was erroneously attributed to not following the process instructions. This was a very valuable lesson. The employee performing the task may very well have the solution to a problem but, for various reasons, may not be willing to voice an opinion. There was a lack of trust and mutual respect that contributed to the failures that caused an increase in costs on a short-term project, leading to potential loss of profits. The engineers were committed to solving the problem, aided by the accounting department raising demanding flags to the leaders. No one asked the employee operating the machine any questions until a consultant was brought on board. This has since changed, and a transition from total quality management to a learning organization was soon implemented.[10]

Business leaders tend to keep their focus on the conservation of resources or the factors of production: land, labor, capital, and entrepreneurship. What is missing is the effect of employee satisfaction on the bottom line.[11] The thrust is that committed employees who function in an environment of mutual respect and trust can contribute directly to the profitability of the transparent organization. The next chapter introduces the Dynamic Strategies Model and further explains how the permeable relationship boundaries contribute to flexibility, while potentially making the organization more responsive to changes in the operating environment and reducing the cost of doing business.

CHAPTER 3

Dynamic Strategies Model

The Dynamic Strategies Model retains the underlying rigor of the traditional linear model but emphasizes the relationship of the elements rather than taking a sequential approach. The boundaries between elements are permeable and can be assigned for development at any level in the organization, depending entirely on the organizational culture and the level of employee empowerment (see Figure 3.1).

In larger organizations, an established spiritual business organization should be in place in order to take maximum advantage of the process, while in smaller organizations, a family-like atmosphere, mutual respect, and trust combine to implement the model quickly. The chief value of this Dynamic Strategies Model is its ability to combine strategic and tactical planning through involving all levels of the organization.

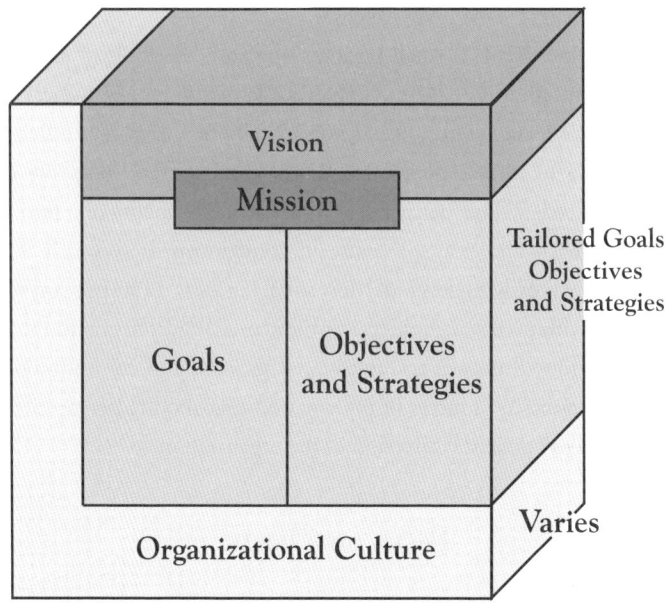

Figure 3.1. Dynamic Strategies Model (© 2010 Seteroff & Campuzano).[1]

Retention of Traditional Approach and Tools

None of the rigor of the traditional linear approach is discarded in the Dynamic Strategies Model. Each of the tools used in the traditional approach has merit and value in this dynamic approach. The tools of analysis can be applied as necessary and at the skill level present within the organization. The time and effort that can be devoted to the development of the strategic plan will dictate the application of the traditional tools.

The strategic planning literature is vast and rigorous. There are many texts readily available, and each has its adherents. The traditional tools of analysis have been developed over many years and each has been found effective to some degree. These tools—like the analysis of strengths, weakness, opportunities, and threats (SWOT), as well as the concept of looking at external environments and internal environments—are easily understood and implemented. Several tools of analysis may be incorporated as resources permit. Where the small business owner determines it is necessary, the application of a more formal set of tools would certainly be appropriate in order to obtain a finer approach.

Reduction of Complexity

From the perspective of a small-business operator, the tools of analysis are often less formal and more intuitive than academic. As small business operators move among clients, suppliers, professional organizations, and employees, they begin to form a perspective of the direction and intensity of the effort that is needed. This perspective may lack the formality of a traditional strategic approach and may be coarse in comparison; however, it is often accurate and less costly to develop. Most small business executives stay in very close contact with their stakeholders and often exchange information through formal and informal networks. Professional societies and community-based organizations are often sources of information that modify perspectives and drive the need to adjust the direction of the organization.

Focus on Clarity

Although the language of strategic planning is often very specific and technical, the focus of the Dynamic Strategies Model is on using brief, clear, and concise language that can be easily understood by all employees. Every employee must be able to do the following:

1. Understand the direction established by vision and mission statements;
2. Understand the goals established for the suborganization;
3. Understand and implement the strategies necessary to achieve the objectives.

The focus is on strategies that achieve the objectives on time, within the established budget and specifications, and that gain acceptance by the customer, client, or user.

Appropriate Business Terminology

Implementation of the Dynamic Strategies Model concentrates on making the language understandable. The strategic and tactical plans created from the application of the model must be brief, clear, and concise in order to be understandable to all stakeholders. If an individual does not understand the plan, he or she is unable to assist in its execution. This is a fine balance because we do not wish to create a plan using language that is insulting to the intelligence of our employees. Some technical language is not only expected but demanded by our employees. Terms that are unique to the industry and are common knowledge are always appropriate, but it may be beneficial to include a section on definitions of terms or phraseology. Words that differ from the dictionary definition, or where the meaning is changed due to the aggregation of the words in a phrase, should also be included in a definitions section. The objective would be to ensure that the plan communicated by the document is clearly understood by every stakeholder. Some technical terminology is necessary, but when clearly explained, the phraseology used may contribute to development of new professional terminology.

The standard business language may vary significantly across business disciplines, as evidenced by the proliferation of acronyms, but the foundational definitions remain similar. All business organizations develop a unique supplemental language that may be clearly understood internally but that may pose a threat to clarity when expanded to other stakeholders. Care must be used to avoid the use of jargon in formal communications because although it may be a part of the culture, it may not translate across strategic business units. Another drawback in using regional colloquiums and other forms of jargon is that they do not translate well across language barriers. In our dynamic, fast-paced operating environment today, many organizations span the globe, with domestic and foreign customers, foreign suppliers, and other diverse stakeholders.

An organization's strategic and tactical plans must be clear and understandable so all can contribute to the success of the organization. In our operating environment today, stakeholders—defined as anyone with an interest in the success of the organization—are often the source of information that assists us in being successful. Sometimes emerging changes come to us from suppliers, customers, or even our competitors. The more people that know, and clearly understand, an organization's strategic plan, the more opportunities there may be for changing and responding effectively.

Project Management Approach

As more organizations—large and small—adopt a project management discipline to accomplish tasks or objectives, the language of project management is entering the mainstream of business. Clear and concise language supports a project management approach with its emphasis on timelines, networks, milestones, tasks, resource allocation, and other success factors. Originally developed as a means of addressing one-time, high-risk endeavors,[2] the discipline has evolved to provide a detailed and efficient way of structuring almost any endeavor while still considering the internal culture.[3] In a true project management approach today, we find a single individual assigned as a project manager, often with a dedicated or shared supporting staff when the risks are high and the endeavor is of high value to the organization.[4] Even smaller organizations have adopted the discipline to the extent that they are able to do so, often without the benefit of a trained, full-time project manager. Project management is assisted by the availability of low-cost project management computer software. Defining the objectives is an essential first step in the process. Once the objectives are clearly identified, the strategies for achieving the objectives in the shortest time possible, and with the least consumption of resources, become a matter of attention to detail in planning.

Goals may have several objectives that are measurable and that will lead toward accomplishing a specific goal. An objective, much like a task under project management, is a discrete statement of work that can be performed by a single individual. The work must be clearly defined and include a predecessor, start time, the technical specifications, the resources available, reporting and coordinating functions, a finish date, and a successor.[5] Once the statement of work is clearly defined, the objective can be assigned to an individual who will be able to determine the strategy for accomplishing the task or objective. In a large organization, this process is usually performed by planners. In small organizations, and in larger organizations with an empowered work force, the individual assigned to perform the task is often allowed to exercise considerable flexibility in determining the strategy for accomplishing the task.

We have long known that the solution to most problems resides at the lowest levels of an organization, generally at a specific employee level. In most cases, a problem is identified by an employee, but the employee is not asked about a potential solution. In an empowered organization, the employee is encouraged to contribute to the solution of emergent problems and is often allowed to take immediate action to resolve an issue rather than delay production. This allows the employee to assume ownership of the solution being implemented and to have a vested interest in its success. In the dynamic strategies approach, the objectives are identified by management but are developed by the employees. When employees are directly involved in the development of the strategies, they assume ownership of the plan and the responsibility for its success. The employee is well aware of the need for coordination and is committed to deliver the task on time, under budget, and to specification.[6] Tracking and reporting of tasks can then be assisted by the use of traditional, cost-effective, project management software tools.

Project Management Tools

Planning, tracking, and metrics are deeply rooted in the discipline of project management. Planning establishes the direction of the project. Tracking involves ensuring that timelines are observed, budget constraints are considered, and technical specifications are met, or exceeded, in order to ensure client acceptance. Metrics are the measuring tools applied to determine progress concerning time, budget, and specification, and are the prime measures of success.

Planning at the beginning of a project is crucial. First, planning establishes the statement of work from which the detailed tasks are derived and the tactical approach is developed. Second, planning presents an opportunity to engage all levels of the organization in applying the best methods, and to examine all possibilities, in reducing the consumption of resources. Third, planning establishes the methodology used for controlling the project and defines the reports that will be used. Many issues are identified through the planning process. Potential contingency measures can be incorporated to assist in reducing the adverse effects of change. Many identified issues can be mitigated, moderated, or resolved during the planning process. The result is a reduction in the risk of failure.[7] Planning contributes to controlling time and resources on a project and produces a closed-loop system. A popular maxim that many project managers cite is, "Failing to plan is planning to fail."[8]

Tracking is an approach used to evaluate, adjust, and make changes to an ongoing project by comparing progress reports against the established project plan. The project manger may opt to implement exception reporting, reporting at specified intervals, budget-based reporting, or another protocol. The key is to identify controls in the plan. Project management is challenging, and there will be unexpected events that may adversely affect the designated controls. Change will happen, and things will go wrong no matter how much planning takes place.[9] Planning for increased time consumption will provide a more flexible schedule. Evaluation, adjustments, and changes create a synergy where the project itself evolves, and there is a clear path to follow. Leaders will then evaluate the situation and choose the best direction.

Using metrics that are common to project management allows the application of proven and robust techniques in evaluating progress. The leader is able to use moderately priced software to track performance against the plan, often in real time. It is not unusual to have access to project planning and reporting across several layers of the organization. Each employee then has the ability to see the supporting detail for each report. GANTT charts (see Figure 3.2) can be used to easily track performance to a planned timeline.

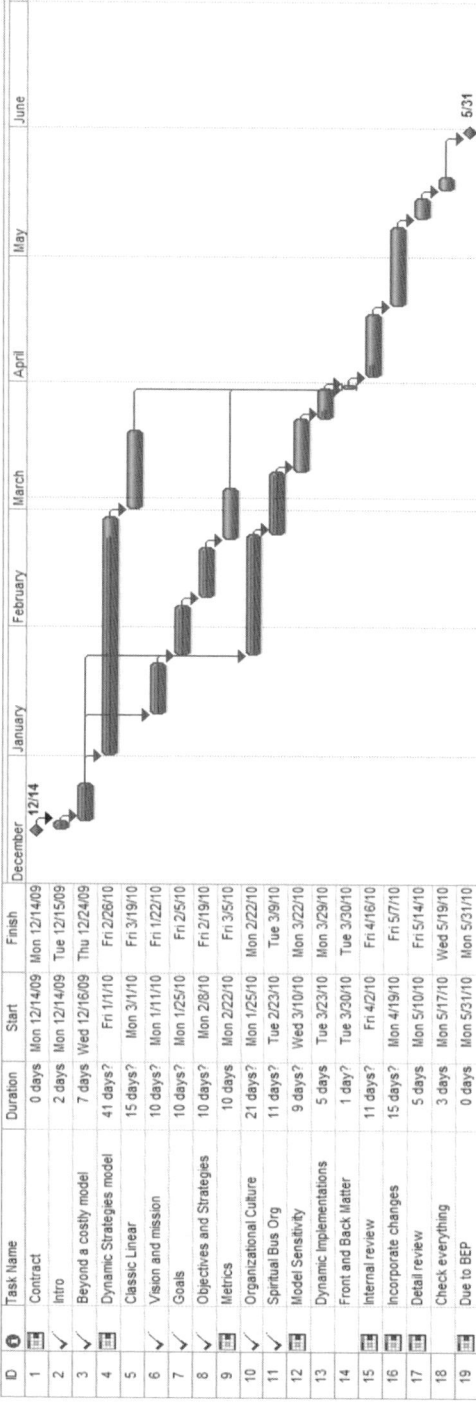

Figure 3.2. Example of GANTT chart developed for this book (as of March 4, 2010).

The graphic presentation allows us to quickly determine if a task is ahead of or behind schedule. Closer examination of the supporting detail can reveal budgetary information. All can compare percentage of budget used with percentage of time consumed, and other measures may be applied. As organizations become more sophisticated in the use of automated project management software, tracking employee performance can be easily tied to the same reporting format. Other tools are certainly available, and today's organization is limited only by the available funds for acquiring sophisticated software and training employees in its use. The purpose of any project management approach is to use metrics to increase the productivity and profitability of the organization.

The question is, how do we know how to measure success at the organizational level? Metrics are the aggregation of tools used to measure success. The most obvious answer is measuring success by profitability. Performance is linked to profitability because it is directly reflected in the cost of doing business. Most other cost factors are common across competitors; therefore, performance is the competitive variable in total cost moderated by employee satisfaction and the level of spirituality present in the organization. Using performance as a tool for measuring success appears to be justified. Other measures of success, including consumer satisfaction and returning consumers, are largely market driven. The drive is to recognize that the entire organization works as a whole to create success. When there is dissonance, even in a single department, the effects may be communicated throughout the organization. Minimizing and addressing issues up front is part of the solution.

Assignment of Responsibility

Use of a project management approach allows planners to develop a statement of work and to assign the work to an individual employee. In a well-organized spiritual business organization, the employee would be engaged in the development of the strategies to achieve the objectives of the task. Having an individual engaged in the development of these strategies will allow the employee to have ownership of the plan. The opportunity to lay blame on superiors is greatly reduced, and the incentive to perform at a higher level is enhanced. In a robust plan, the employee assists in developing the metrics associated with performance, contributes to the plan, and is directly responsible for its successful implementation. As Richard Hodgetts stated, what gets measured gets done. When an employee is directly involved in defining the strategies for achieving particular objectives, the satisfactory conclusion of the task results in greater personal satisfaction. When employees are satisfied in the workplace, and when a level of commitment is attained, productivity increases, as does satisfaction and trust. An increase in employee satisfaction and trust, along with improved productivity, results in a reduction of the cost of doing business and an increase in profitability.

Permeable Boundaries

The strength of the Dynamic Strategies Model is that the boundaries are permeable. We do not have to go from one area of the model to another in any specific order. Clearly, the vision statement is the prerogative of the chief executive officer (CEO), and the mission statement remains the purview of the president or other head of a strategic business unit. However, the goals can be established at any managerial level of the organization, and the objectives may be established very low in the organizational structure. The strategies to achieve the objectives, or tasks in a project management environment, are best developed by the employee who will be asked to perform the work. The employee who develops the strategies must have a clear understanding of both the mission and vision statements as well as the goal that the specific task is designed to achieve. Conversely, the manager developing the goals must have a good grasp of the capabilities of the employees and their ability to develop the strategies to achieve the objectives. The strength of this model is that the vision begins at the top, but the strategies to achieve the objectives could well be driven by the employee. Driving the strategies from the employee level could mean that the manager may change the goals—as long as the goals remain in consonance with the mission and vision statements. If the strategic changes are successfully implemented, they may result in the need to revise the vision and mission statements. This is an example of Richard Hodgetts's statement—in any conflict between vision and culture, culture will win. Leaders who choose to ignore the possibility that culture may change the organizational direction may find that their organizations are less profitable.

Change in Operational Environment

When employees are empowered to develop the strategies necessary to achieve certain objectives, the organizational culture allows the empowerment to extend to making adjustments in the statement of work. Based on emergent changes in the operational environment, the organization can respond quickly and effectively. Empowerment reflects acceptance of risk. Change is neither good nor bad. The response to change in the operating environment separates a responsive organization from a static organization. The response may take several directions. In a traditional organization, employees who notice a change report the specifics to their supervisor, and the information is passed up the chain of command until it reaches the individual with decision-making authority. The difficulty arises when the information received by the individual with this authority loses detail due to the several iterations. Some large organizations take the approach of simply endorsing the original notification with their recommendation before passing it on to the next individual in line. This procedure reflects the character of the observation, but the time required to reach the decision maker may be unacceptable from a competitive perspective. Empowerment is providing some level of decision-making authority, albeit a limited one, to the employee who notices a change in the operational environment. Empowerment, therefore, allows quick response to changes in the operating environment at some level of risk. The decision then becomes a timely response, which is more desirable than exposure to risk resulting from a decision made at a lower level.

Change From Multiple Directions

Businesses, large or small, are influenced by a global marketplace. Change is driven from multiple directions. Business survival is dependent on rapidly adapting to change in the operating environment. Change is uncomfortable and contains elements of risk (see Figure 3.3), but failure to change may mean the demise of the business.

Resistance to change is supported by fear, whether the fear is real or imagined. Change can be resisted since traditional formularies have worked in the past, but in a global market, change is fast. Failure to recognize change poses a risk for continuity of operations. Recognition of the need to change

Figure 3.3. Cloud of change (© 2010 Campuzano & Seteroff).

but failure to respond quickly and appropriately may be as detrimental to
success as failure to recognize the need to change at all. Stakeholders may
not agree with the responses to changes in the operating environment, but
if included in the dialogue, stakeholders will find the response to change
understandable. Recognizing the need to change, and involving all stakeholders in the decision process, will determine the degree of acceptability.
Simple complacency is comfortable but will hinder change, and appropriate change has a positive effect on the organization.

Internal and External Change

Change is driven from many directions and the benefits of change may
be dynamic, as the entire organization is involved. Change creates new
challenges and brings new life to a stagnant organization. New ideas and

brainstorming sessions start a wave of enthusiasm and new prospects for the future. New challenges arise with change. The challenges may be foreseen or unforeseen, but the leaders of the organization must rise to meet the emergent challenges and the new changes. A key element is to communicate the importance of precision in the resolution of changes. The leaders, and mainly the managers who set the changes into action, facilitate transparent change. Transparency allows seamless communication of the responsive actions throughout the organization.

New changes are readily accepted when the leaders are inspired and they convey the enthusiasm for change to the employees. Resistance to change appears to be inherent; however, the resistance to change becomes invalidated with positive attitudes from leaders, managers, and employees. The hope of implementing a new system that is increasingly functional, practical, and profitable for the organization is embedded in the desire for change. Inspired leaders motivate and bring a level of enthusiasm, along with a desire to change, to the employees. Change then becomes the new challenge accepted by all.

Teamwork at all levels is important to the success of change. A synergy is created throughout the organization so that the changes become part of the organization's culture. Building a specific team that interacts within the organization will facilitate the implementation of the changes and further provide an assurance that the changes will achieve the desired objectives. The specific team assigned is empowered to answer questions, investigate options, provide direction in designing a smooth transition, and retain the flexibility necessary to respond effectively.

The leaders empower employees to implement changes, and a new transformational organizational culture emerges (see Figure 3.4). Change is a constant within a progressive organization. Building an organizational culture where change is the expected norm designs a culture of change. Leaders must be aware that managers must continue to respond to incremental change driven by internal metrics, while leaders concurrently apply the quantum change in responding to external factors. Change is productive, but there must be a balanced approach since too much change may result in a counterproductive environment. When changes become the norm, employees might implement the change half-heartedly, and this is a danger to be avoided. Leaders must consider the change, consider the

Figure 3.4. Rays of change (© 2010 Campuzano & Seteroff).

value of the change, and evaluate the effectiveness the change will bring. Too many changes can be as detrimental to the organization as no change at all. An emerging transformational organization results from successful implementation of responsiveness to changes in the external environment. A dynamic organization that has evaluated the risk of change and that has implemented the correct tools for the employees to achieve the desired changes makes for a successful transformational culture.

Acceptance of response to change becomes a part of the competitive advantage enjoyed by an organization. Designing a niche within the organizational culture that fluctuates with the market and that changes the ebb and flow of the operating environment is desirable for sustaining a competitive advantage. The leaders of the organization are responsible for a continued evaluation of the external environment. This is where a "SWOT analysis," along with other tools, is helpful to the organization. The evaluation of SWOT—that is, strengths, weaknesses, opportunities, and threats—presented in the following chapter is crucial. A spiritual business organization generates business as a competitive advantage that diminishes some of the risks inherent in change. The importance is to generate a competitive advantage by fostering an ability to have all levels of the organization identify changes in the operating environment. Empowering all levels of the organization to recognize the needed change allows for the development of strategies to meet the challenge and to deploy the solution for the benefit of the organization.

Communication Essentials

The strength of a dynamic strategic process is the ability to present a plan to all stakeholders in a brief, clear, and concise manner. As the plan is being generated, it moves throughout the organization and is modified, as necessary, by the individuals that have control over its execution. For example, the chief executive officer first develops the vision statement. Next, the mission statement is added to the vision statement by the head of each strategic business unit. The product may be exchanged with other strategic business units so that collaborative ventures may take place or simply for information. The strategic business unit executive will then distribute the plan to subordinates, who will develop the goals necessary to achieve the vision and mission statements. The executives developing the goals may choose to collaborate on some goals that are of mutual interest; however, most goals are developed within the suborganization. The executives will then pass the goals, along with the vision and mission statements, to a project management team to develop a statement of work or to staff to develop objectives by management. Once the objectives or tasks are defined, it is appropriate to engage the employees who will be performing the tasks in order to take advantage of the detailed knowledge that resides within the individuals' expertise. Once resources are identified for each individual task, or objective, it is recorded in the form of a revised statement of work. The statement of work can be assigned to the individual assisting in its development and then integrated into a formal plan. Assistance from other organizations may be identified, and these would be negotiated with the organization that will be providing support. As tasks are aggregated into a plan, predecessors and successors are identified for the best utilization of resources.

The advantage of a dynamic strategic plan that is brief, clear, and concise is that it can be easily understood across all levels of the organization and applied at a tactical level. Since the plan is essentially written by the employees that will execute the plan, the language should be easily understood. As the plan is passed up the line, it is aggregated with other plans to form a cohesive whole. This allows supervisors, managers, and executives to clearly understand the work to be performed in their areas of responsibility. Since the employee who will be performing the task essentially writes the task, clarity is not an issue. The employee understands what needs to be done and communicates this to the supervisor. The supervisor is able to determine the resources required and summarizes the needs to managers. The managers are able to allocate resources appropriately, due to the clarity of the descriptions. With modern project management tools, the plan developed in this manner may be summarized, but it should still provide the ability to look at specifics when necessary. This dynamic approach allows leadership characteristics to be exercised at any level of the organization from the employee performing the task to the chief executive officer.

Leadership at All Levels

The leadership of the organization becomes a shared task when leaders empower employees to take on leadership roles. Emergent leadership can only take place in an environment where empowerment and self-actualization is promoted. The organizational culture permeates all levels of the organization from the chief executive to the newest employee, and leadership becomes a shared commodity. While the leaders of the organization remain in their designated roles, employees are empowered to share leadership responsibilities as the emergent situation dictates. Self-actualization and self-governance empowers employees to take on leadership roles, while leaders remain secure. This acceptance of distributive leadership allows for the development of a culture of quick response to emergent change, creating a *leader-full* organization.[10]

Authentic leadership is defined as leading with honesty and integrity.[11] Leading with the heart[12] is to lead with honesty, integrity, compassion, cognition, and love.[13] This is the link between business and what some might consider soft science, yet there is no fluff. These characteristics of leadership support an organizational culture that is based on understanding and empowering employees.

Empowerment supports emergent leadership. Emergent leaders are informal leaders who come into a position of leadership when a situation occurs that requires their specific skill, human expertise, or technical knowledge to respond rapidly to change. The informal leader is not appointed but takes on a leadership role based on a great desire to accomplish the tasks for the benefit of the organization. An emergent leader is one who the rest of the employees will follow regardless of their relative position. This concept resembles followership, where we recognize that the best follower is a leader that voluntarily subordinates themselves for the good of the organization, mission, or task.[14] This concept is similar to self-governance, where the employees will create an organizational subculture in which each employee is responsible for their tasks and actions.[15] The subculture facilitates informal leaders to take leadership roles and to resolve emergent issues without having to escalate the decision.

A culture of empowerment supports a subculture where employees are encouraged to make decisions that affect the work environment. These decisions deal with everyday issues but may include decisions to change an existing process to accommodate change in the operating environment. This approach, when based on a clear understanding of the plan, provides a quick response in order to remain competitive. The dynamic strategies approach provides a tool to communicate a plan that supports rational decision making with integrity.

Empowering decision making by employees at all levels of the organization can provide an increased level of competitiveness when the strategic plan is communicated effectively and the desired direction is clear. In a spiritual business organization, the potential for a breach of law or ethics is minimized. The area of concern would be relegated to the areas where legal and ethical issues are not in consonance. On examining Figure 3.5, we can see that if a decision is both ethical and legal, there is no issue in any organization. If a decision were not legal and not ethical, a well-structured business organization that is not engaged in illegal activity by design would have no issue in rejecting the decision. Where the spiritual business organization with a well-communicated strategic plan would see decision-making benefits is in the areas between legal and ethical. In global operations, it is entirely conceivable that ethical considerations in one area would not

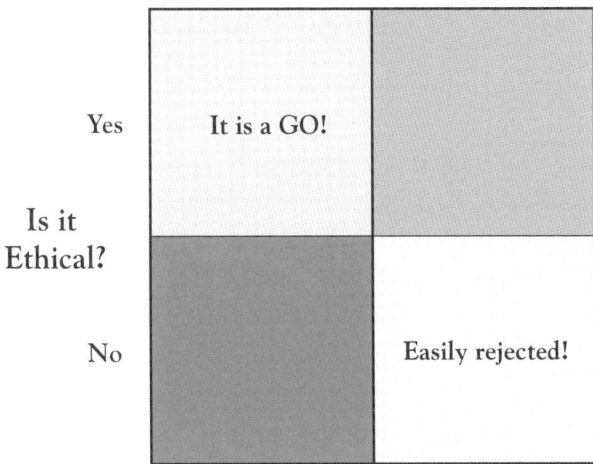

	Yes	It is a GO!	

Figure 3.5. Ethical decision-making matrix (© 2001 Seteroff; © 2010 Seteroff & Campuzano).

necessarily translate well into other areas. Laws differ, and, in general, the laws of the country in which the organization is located would be the operative laws that must be observed. Employees who are operating remotely, or who must modify the existing process directives due to emergent changes, may be empowered to make decisions that are in consonance with the strategic and tactical plan without placing the organization in jeopardy.

Spiritualized leadership transcends authentic leadership and leading from the heart because it involves a deeper level of commitment from the leader. The implementation of self-actualization, self-governance, a learning environment, and a holistic approach to problem solving would be the reward. The leader is able to empower employees to rise to any challenge by providing opportunities to improve skills and knowledge to enhance a balanced life. Motivation, commitment, and leading with passion are characteristics of the spiritualized leader. Passion is to lead with enthusiasm, and this may be described as a heart on fire. Passion is as hot as burning coals, and passion is transmitted by exemplary behavior. There is increased interest in becoming an exceptional leader and leading employees to a greater awareness with education, knowledge, professional development, and personal development. Spiritualized leadership is more than a title and more than a leadership style: it is a way of life. Spirituality becomes an extension into the work environment. With the advent of the Internet, work and home intertwine—leaders take work home and home is taken to the office.

Cultural Drivers

The organizational culture surrounds the Dynamic Strategies Model. The culture of an organization does not stand alone. Culture is influenced internally by the employees and externally by the stakeholders, including all members of the supply chain and distribution network as well as the customers. Internally, the organizational culture is driven by the local, regional, national, and global culture of its employees. This is augmented by the culture established by the organization as it continues in existence. The external culture is also driven by local, regional, national, and global factors. The closer the relationships between the employees of an organization and the stakeholders are, the closer aligned the cultures will become. In crafting the vision statement, the chief executive officer would do well to pay close attention to the culture of the organization and how that culture interacts with the organizational cultures of suppliers, distributors, and the customers. The closer the cultures are aligned, the greater the probability of collecting actionable information from outside the organization in time to respond to emergent change.

Although the culture may vary across several organizations comprising the operational environment of the firm, the Dynamic Strategies Model is sensitive to change because it is a model that empowers every employee. Strategic business units operating across several countries or regions are empowered to adapt to the cultural mores of the area in which they operate. Understanding that several cultures may be operational simultaneously allows greater clarity in decision-making authority to be exercised by individuals. For example, decision-making authority may be at the task level in one area but elevated to a supervisory level in another. Empowerment of employees may be selective and may differ from organization to organization as the cultural differences dictate.

The effect of culture on an organization, and the ability of the executives to recognize and adapt their thinking to take advantage of the differences in cultural mores, is at the heart of the dynamic strategic model. When organizational culture is considered during the decision-making process, the likelihood of developing an organization that is sensitive to change, and that is willing to act on emergent change for the benefit of the organization, is increased. Culture, therefore, is the foundation of a dynamic strategies process.

CHAPTER 4

Classical Linear Method

The classical linear model is a proven design, it is vigorous, and it supports a zero-based approach with subsequent revisions. Traditionally, the classical approach has required considerable training to implement, and the larger the company, the larger the staff required to perform the background analysis leading to a robust strategic plan. Strategic planning is effective only when it is detailed, and it is usually approved at the highest levels of an organization. The difficulty arises in the implementation phase because the plan is voluminous and uses technical language.

A strategic plan developed in the traditional manner is a result of considerable data gathering, analysis, and negotiation both internally and externally.[1] The data gathering can be rather intense, the tools of analysis can be complex, and the process can be time-consuming, requiring highly skilled and well-trained individuals. For large organizations with the means to support a full-time strategic planning team, the classical linear method remains the best choice.

Holistic Approach

The modern classic linear model is well established and is based on the logistics planning used during World War II.[2] The process has matured and has become a holistic approach that takes into consideration all aspects of an organization, including operations, marketing, human resources, financial factors, and administration. Larger organizations would have a strategic planning department, consisting of one or more individuals from each of the disciplines. Each individual would be well versed in their discipline but would also have training in the analytical techniques demanded by robust strategic planning. Each individual would work in concert with other members of the team to develop a holistic strategic plan.

Traditional Approach

The team approach is to develop a strategic plan beginning with the vision statement from the chief executive officer (CEO) and a mission statement from the senior executive of the strategic business unit. Based on the vision and mission statements, the team gathers information from internal and external sources, commercial and government resources, and within the industry in which the organization operates, both domestically and internationally. Gathering data on competitors takes priority because accurate placement of the organization within the sector of operations becomes important. This initial data collection can be time-consuming and costly. Frequently, consultants are hired to address specific areas within their area of expertise. Where the organization has the capability, consultants are retained only when necessary so that confidentiality is maintained.

Many large organizations have developed their own tools of analysis. However, as discussed in Chapter 3, one common tool is SWOT (strengths, weakness, opportunities, and threats) analysis, which examines the internal factors of strengths and weaknesses versus the external factors of opportunities and threats. The basic SWOT model has undergone several refinements, but it remains a foundational model of analysis. The basic SWOT model has been expanded to a 9-cell model to provide a middle ground and a 12-cell model to provide greater differentiation. The 12-cell model has been developed with creative application of pie shapes to assist in presenting a complex analysis in graphic form. Complex computer-based software has been developed and modified internally by large organizations to fit the models of analysis favored by their company's executives.

Proven in Practice

The traditional approach has been proven in practice over several decades. The benefits of this traditional approach to strategic planning are well established in the business community. The leaders of small organizations usually express a desire to implement the practices that have been successful. This sometimes leads organizations to develop a plan without adequate preparation and with limited resources. The lack of internal resources has spurred the availability of a multitude of consulting firms dedicated to providing strategic management services. The main draw-back to this approach for small business is the cost of developing a strategic plan in the traditional manner.

Essential Baseline

The traditional approach should be used to develop a baseline for any organization, large or small. The discipline of data collection and the tools used for analysis remains the same regardless of the size of the organization. Professional societies and industry organizations frequently provide a considerable amount of industry and regulatory information to their members. This information can provide a good foundation for narrowing the scope of the analysis to the specific area of operations. The more detailed and extensive the data collection process becomes, the more robust the analysis and the better the baseline plan. In larger organizations, this baseline is crucial because all future plans are merely modifications of the original baseline—unless a zero-based approach is implemented.

Zero-Based Approach

A zero-based approach, although lengthy and costly, is essential for large organizations to establish a sound foundation upon which a strategic plan can be developed. Small businesses should also consider a zero-based approach for their initial strategic plan if funds are available. Once the initial plan is established, the plan is traditionally revised either annually or biannually. A zero-based approach disregards existing knowledge and assumes a starting position of a blank slate. The data collection phase is extensive and generally includes historical aspects as well as collecting data on current operations in the business sector. The larger the organization, the more extensive the support required to generate a zero-based strategic and tactical plan. The zero-based approach is always lengthy and has a high initial cost, but it often results in lower revision costs. The benefit of reducing costs for subsequent revisions, and the cost savings, is extended to implementation, and this often results in a lower life-cycle cost.[1]

A zero-based approach is undertaken for two reasons—first, as an initial foundation to develop a strategic plan, and second, when the existing strategic plan has proven to be ineffective and updates to an existing plan are not acceptable. In the first case, understanding the internal and external operating environments is important before a strategy can be formulated for the organization. The zero-based approach determines where the organization is positioned at that moment in time. Knowing where the organization is in relation to its competitors and the market allows the formulation of a robust strategic and tactical plan.

Resorting to a zero-based approach may be the only avenue remaining when the current strategic plan is found to be ineffective. In this case, the classical linear model allows leaders to suspend what is already known and proceed to evaluating the internal and external environments without the bias of existing knowledge. This is a very difficult concept for those who have been primarily responsible for the development of upgrades to the strategic plan. For this reason, a zero-based approach, under conditions of a strategic plan failure, are usually relegated to consultants or assigned to a specially convened internal team reporting directly to the senior executive ordering the zero-based approach. Access to all organizational data is essential, so a strong confidentiality agreement must be in place or internal resources must be utilized. Internal teams may require assistance from a specialized consulting firm.

Lengthy Process

The zero-based approach begins with the assumption that any data currently available is invalid. Every piece of information is suspect. All information must be corroborated, to the extent feasible, from internal or external sources, preferably from external sources that are not tainted by politically correct interpretations. The rule of thumb is that for every single data point, there must be at least two supporting corroborative pieces of evidence. Obtaining the data in the usual course of preparation is routine; however, searching out the supporting evidence and resolving any resulting conflicts lengthens the process considerably.

Engaging in a zero-based approach is a very exacting and complex undertaking that must be considered carefully. The zero-based approach is a team-based endeavor, using skilled and well-educated employees under the leadership of a trusted executive. It is essential to have full access to all organizational information and a license to pursue an investigation in any direction deemed appropriate for developing a strong foundation upon which to create a strategic plan. Adequate support in the form of research capability must be available, and there must be no constraints placed upon the time or effort required by the team.

High Initial Cost

The initial cost of a zero-based approach is disproportionately high. The individuals involved are generally well educated, always highly skilled, and tend to work long hours, so are usually compensated at a higher rate than others of an equal skill level. Physical support would include a secure place in which to work, computer equipment, access to databases, and access to periodicals. Support often also extends to membership in professional societies that may assist in providing, or developing, data of interest to the organization. The time required to develop a strategic plan using the traditional linear approach is lengthy, and the support required to ensure that all developed data are assimilated and evaluated appropriately tends to escalate the cost. The zero-based approach is jokingly referred to as a program that never ends, requires an endless amount of resources, and provides a plan that few will read and understand.

Moderate Update Cost

The benefit of the zero-based approach is that once implemented, the cost to update it on an annual or biannual basis is moderate. Because the zero-based approach is so detailed, and so well supported, it is only necessary to revisit the original references. A competent researcher should be able to determine if there is new information available using a word, or theme, search in the databases that were originally consulted. Internal data can be structured so that any changes are highlighted, and it is therefore readily available to the team generating the update. The update periodicity must also be carefully considered against the cost of performing the update, and this should be balanced against the velocity of the operating environment in which the organization engages. Most large organizations settle on an annual revision; however, in slower-moving sectors a biannual revision is not unusual. Higher-velocity sectors may find semiannual revisions to be more appropriate. Although the costs to update the strategic plan are relatively moderate, the update is a specialized area of endeavor.

Strategic Planning Team

The zero-based approach is a very specialized effort that is not lightly undertaken because of its lengthy duration and high associated costs. The strategic planning team is usually multidisciplinary, consisting of well-educated and highly skilled individuals from each of the several disciplines comprising the organization. The team is headed by an executive that enjoys the trust of the chief executive officer. Once in place, this organization will usually continue to operate as a team, meeting periodically throughout the year, with a dedicated surge of effort, when required, to update the plan. The periodic meetings throughout the year are designed to exchange information on scanning the internal and external environments within the specific discipline. The new data is considered by other members of the team in order to determine how the emergent information must be applied to gain a better understanding in their own areas of expertise. The team will convene in dedicated effort to update the strategic plan so that a viable tactical response can be generated, either on schedule or in response to a change in the operating environment. The decision to update the strategic plan is usually made by the chief executive officer in consultation with all executives responsible for the execution of the plan.

Top-Down Decisions

The decision to participate in a zero-based strategic planning initiative is sufficiently resource intensive, so as to justify the direct involvement of the chief executive officer or a senior executive in a strategic business unit. In a classic linear approach, the chief executive officer begins the process, and all efforts are aimed at supporting the vision statement. In a classical linear approach, the flow is unidirectional, albeit with feedback loops at each stage to ensure that the previous direction is adhered to. The classic linear approach is a top-down effort.

The top-down effort is suitable for large organizations, and this approach may be used for small organizations as long as the employees are operating in a directed mode. This approach is not useful in very small, team-based or more collaborative organizations. Small business organizations of two or three individuals are either totally directive or highly collaborative. In a highly directive organization, a strategic plan is not necessarily communicated. In a collaborative organization, the communication of the direction and the clear understanding of the desires of the owner or chief executive officer are absolutely essential. As the collaborative organization begins to grow, the need to continue the communication becomes critical to the success of the organization as a whole. When the employees remain empowered, and continue to operate in a collaborative manner, it is essential that the direction is clear. The authority to make decisions in the presence of change should be in consonance with the vision and mission statements. The vision and mission statements must be clearly understood by all. The limits of authority should be clearly communicated and well documented. Regardless of the size of the organization, and the area in which it operates, the chief executive officer remains responsible.

CHAPTER 5

Vision and Mission

The terms *vision* and *mission* have been used almost interchangeably, but their meaning depends on the author and the work. The vision and mission statements of an organization have clear distinctions but work together as a whole. What is essential is the ability to differentiate between the enterprise level and the strategic business level. In plain language, the *vision* represents the dream, and the *mission* is the path to get there. For our purposes, we will adopt the term *vision* as being used at the enterprise level and *mission* as being appropriate at the strategic business level. For example, the General Electric Company, or another similar large conglomerate, has the corporate vision, "GE: imagination at work,"[1] but there are separate mission statements for the entity that manufactures light bulbs[2] and the entity that manufactures jet engines.[3] The point is that each of the subordinate companies is engaged in a different area, so the missions would be different but are still in consonance with the vision established by the chief executive officer of the corporation. At the small-business level, even in the smallest of organizations, the vision would be a long-range statement that would encompass several areas of endeavor, but each area of interest could have a separate mission statement. For very small organizations, one or the other would be required but probably not both.

Vision

Vision, as used here, is the dream of where the organization would be in the distant future. In North American and European organizations, this may be several decades or years, but in a practical sense, a vision changes with chief executive officers, so the operational term is generally shorter than a decade, although it is not the limitation established by the new officer. In some Asian conglomerates, the vision may extend for a century or more under the operational approach that the company may not know what the world will be like in a century, but it is expected that the company will still be there as a viable entity. The vision of the organization will have changed along the way to meet the demands of the changing operational environment. An excellent example of this from the North American experience is the vision of the railroad system in the early half of the 20th century, which saw itself as being in the railroad business instead of in the transportation industry. This narrow view was inappropriate, and as other modes of transportation became prominent, several railroads were not in a position to take advantage of the opportunities. Even as railroads began to fail, they were assimilated into the more affluent railroad organizations that took over the routes and equipment but still retained the direction of moving freight and passengers by rail.

What does vision mean in the real sense? Let us look at a small organization and a start-up organization of one individual. In a small organization that offers consulting services with a few employees, the opportunity arises to expand the business beyond the consulting practice by a client requesting that the organization take on a turnkey responsibility. Specifically, a small engineering-based consulting firm recommends the implementation of an approach that requires integration of hardware, software, and processes in response to an engagement to address an identified issue in meeting contractual requirements. The client accepts the recommendation and, since a high level of trust had been established, requests that the consulting firm continues in implementing the recommendations. The chief executive of the small business has the option of hiring someone else or, perhaps applying the lessons of the railroads, expanding the business to incorporate new strategic business units to deliver on the emergent contract. If the vision does not cover the opportunity, the decision could very well be to avoid the risk and to share the contract with another organization. That would certainly pose less risk; however, it avoids taking advantage of the opportunity. The small business owner could simply expand to include hardware and software strategic business units by generating new mission statements and devising a vision statement that covers not only the existing and new opportunities but one that also allows sufficient latitude so that an opportunity in the future would not be rejected. This allows expansion of the business, spreads the risk, and allows for potential sale of the new strategic business units.

Let us look at a small business owner who is starting a quilting business because she enjoys quilting and believes she could do a better job at machine quilting than what is available in the area. For her, the new business is a means of acquiring a commercial-grade quilting machine and taking in quilting work serves to pay for her own hobby by offering the quilting services to others. Very clearly, this is a personal desire and a good way to justify the cost of a machine while obtaining discounts on fabric, batting, thread, and notions as a business owner in the trade. Then an amazing transformation takes place: the quilting services come into ever-increasing demand as the quality of the work is recognized, and the owners' faith in herself is justified. The additional exposure creates a demand for her to teach quilting at the shops that previously collected the quilts for her and delivered the finished product. Now a new opportunity beckons, and the time demand becomes split. Here is an opportunity to make a decision on hiring an employee or bringing in a partner with a similar skill and work ethic.

Enterprise Level

We cannot predict where our organization will be in the future because the further out we look, the fuzzier the future becomes. We must be careful to establish a vision that strikes a balance. This balance is very difficult to achieve because we must not only establish a direction but also ensure that the direction aligns with the organizational culture. As Richard Hodgetts stated in an address to Nova Southeastern doctoral students at the 1996 Academy of Management, "In any conflict between vision and culture, culture will win." At the same time, the direction must be clear enough and stated in such a manner as to be able to provide guidance to a reasonably astute employee in the absence of specific policy. This enterprise vision statement should be brief, clear, and concise enough to be understood across all levels of the organization. The vision must be easily applied in both (a) the development of a mission statement by subordinate strategic business units, and (b) the individual employee faced with changes in the operating environment not covered by specific policy or organizational guidelines. Mainly, the vision statement must be understandable and implementable.

One current example of a vision comes from the November 2009 announcement by The Coca-Cola Company,[4] which stated, "'2020 Vision and Roadmap for Winning Together' builds upon the Company's mission to refresh the world and inspire moments of optimism and happiness, while creating value for shareowners and making a difference across the globe." The announcement continues to offer goals that were generated in collaboration with stakeholders.

Small Consulting Firm

On a smaller scale, the vision statement of a small consulting firm providing project management and front-end logistics services was simply stated as, "Provide value to make the client successful."[5] The rationale was that if the client was successful, the organization providing the services would also be successful. The number of clients the organization had were few but intensely loyal, largely as a result of the effort to provide quality service and the employees being empowered to make decisions to accommodate changes in the operating environment. Because the number of employees and subcontractors were few, and the subcontractors were all individuals, control by the owner was not compromised.

Single-Person Operation

In a single-person operation, the vision is frequently informal at best, and not recorded, but is generally consistent over several years. A specific single-person operation is used in this example. The owner of the small quilting business repeatedly stated that she was "doing what [was] fun and getting paid for it." The emphasis was on enjoying the hobby that had turned into a viable business that was quickly recognized as providing a quality service at a reasonable cost. When the owner raised the rates in an attempt to reduce the backlog over the holidays, the customers continued with no reduction in volume. An interesting aside is that in an informal conversation with the owner-operator, she decided to retain the higher rates for her work for the coming year, and the number of customers and the number of quilts per customer increased. As the owner-operator stopped having fun and expanded into teaching, the vision of personal enjoyment continued.

Start-Up Consultancy

A current start-up consultancy consisting of a single owner identified the following vision statement, "Courage to become; Strength to be more." The idea was to first design a logo that represented the values of the consultancy business, and, after careful thought, a lion was chosen for courage and strength. New endeavors generally reflect the specific desires of the entrepreneur and pull at the core of one's being to reach the highest human potential. To reach the highest human potential is at the core of spirituality. Building a business that promotes self-efficacy and a supportive organizational culture provides an experience where employees are driven by both internal motives and a supportive organizational culture.[6] Individuals who perform a task with confidence are persistent in their endeavors and perform better.

Direction by Chief Executive Officer

The important issue regarding the formulation of a vision statement is that the owner or chief executive officer is the person responsible for determining the direction. The pitfall is to ensure that the vision statement is clear enough to be readily understood, broad enough to allow flexibility, and the direction specific enough to be applied by all levels of the organization when faced with a change in the operating environment that is not covered by traditional policy. It remains a feature of the Dynamic Strategies Model that culture permeates all boundaries, including the vision, to ensure that whatever direction is established by the chief executive officer can be supported by the organizational culture.

Alignment With Culture

It is no accident that the representation of culture wraps around the Dynamic Strategies Model to present a mutual boundary for all elements of the model. Culture, in the original model developed by Edward Pierce, was the foundation of the model; however, in the Dynamic Strategies Model, culture is all-encompassing. Culture becomes the basis for all decisions as tools of analysis are applied in the context of the organizational culture. An example of how culture manifests itself in the creation

of vision is the large number of organizations that succumbed to the fla-
vor-of-the-month business strategy of the 1980s, where every successful
chief executive officer wrote a book on how to succeed and provided a
prescriptive approach. The books have great historical value as cases, and
lessons could certainly be learned from the described process. However,
many organizations simply adopted the prescription in anticipation of a
similar success that could not materialize for the following reasons:

1. The prescription had already been applied, and the company had
   moved on to something different.
2. Others were also implementing the same approach.
3. There was little attention paid to the culture of the organization, let
   alone to the culture of the stakeholders.

The organizational culture becomes imperative since the vision of the
company is the driver of the organizational culture. When the culture
cannot support the vision, the guidance provided by the vision will
be ignored. The lack of integration of the vision by the organizational
culture can be devastating since it commences a downward spiral of ill
effects for the entire organization. Informal leaders within the organization are capable of bringing devastation into the culture by their failure to
support the vision. An important aspect to note is that management may
be responsible for the decline of the organizational culture by permitting
informal leaders to continue with devious behavior, and by not stopping
the behavior, the management then becomes responsible for contributing to the chaos. The vision is completely lost in the chaos and adversely
affects the organization as a whole. The effects are felt at individual performance levels, leading to a reduction in profitability. The culture manifests specific characteristics representative of the employees. The values
and attitudes of each employee, supervisor, manger, and executive combine to create a unique organizational culture. A small business can have
several subcultures operational within the larger culture, but the organizational culture is composed of all of the employees within the company
and can be considered to be a living, breathing entity.

Mission

The mission in the Dynamic Strategies Model is derived from the vision statement but must be in consonance with the direction of the organization. Although small organizations with a single strategic business unit may only need the vision or mission statement, both are more appropriate because where the vision establishes a long-term direction, the mission statement can be more focused on the line of business. When both are in place, the organization empowers its employees to expand their horizons and to take advantage of emergent opportunities that may be outside the business-related scope of the mission statement. As we saw in the General Electric example, *imagination at work*[7] allows the strategic business units the flexibility to move beyond the present to take advantage of innovations. The same can be applied to even the smallest business unit.

Strategic Business Unit

In business, most of us learn that we cannot do everything well. That is why companies tend to specialize in the areas of their core competencies,[8] just as we see cross-disciplinary and multidisciplinary efforts become more collaborative. In the highly competitive, often global, operational environment we face today, doing one thing best is often more effective than doing several things well. Having made that statement, we must still leave room for the generalist[9] who can pull all these diverse elements together into a marketable product. A strategic business unit will have a limited focus and concentrate on its core competencies to do few things, or even one single thing, best. The question then becomes, how do we integrate the emergent technologies and processes to ensure a competitive advantage is captured and maintained? Leaders of strategic business units must then balance the operational changes using a managerial approach in order to allow the luxury to contemplate the quantum changes to the organization that is within the domain of the leader.[10]

Established Strategic Business Unit Leader

Depending on the size of the parent entity and the organizational structure, the strategic business unit leader can be the president, an executive vice president, or some other title. However, the single requirement is that the title must include the ability to legally bind the company contractually. In larger organizations with a parent company, the title would usually be that of president. However, if the subsidiary is independently traded, it may be a portfolio item of a holding company, and the function is relatively independent. This chapter will not address a holding company asset but limits the discussion to a company under the direction of the vision of a parent organization.

President

The title of *president* of a strategic business unit will be assumed to represent a level of independence within the charter of the strategic business unit, with bottom-line responsibility to the parent organization. This is the individual responsible for establishing the mission of the strategic business unit and ensuring that the mission is in alignment with the vision statement of the parent organization. The organizational structure is usually independent, although common software and processes may be in place to ensure compatibility. The strategic business unit otherwise functions relatively independently, with its own business development and operations responsibilities.

Executive Vice President

A strategic business unit headed by an executive vice president would not necessarily have the autonomy to function independently and would probably receive administrative support from the parent organization. The executive vice president would probably be limited to operations with business development as well as research and development, with other nonoperational functions being performed by the parent organization. Whether the strategic business unit would have its own mission statement or adopt a modified version of the vision statement is not clear. However, it is clear that alignment with the organization's culture is essential for success.

Alignment of Culture

Whether the mission statement is developed independently or in collaboration with the parent organization, the mission statement must be in consonance with the organization's vision and must align with the organizational culture of the strategic business unit. The employees of the strategic business unit must identify with, and support, the mission statement at the visceral level. The mission statement should be able to provide guidance when existing policy directives, work rules, and process instructions do not cover an emergent issue. A good example can be drawn from the military, where members will brave their own safety and ignore censure from superiors to extricate a comrade from a tenuous position. The culture dictates the action even when the policy dictates otherwise. The same can be found in some established work teams that are accustomed to working independently, where—even though the policy does not allow the use of overtime—an employee will work through the night to resolve an unexpected problem because the schedule calls for the next phase to commence in the morning. The culture demands the extra effort. This culture can only be sustained in the long term when supervisors understand, and become a part of, the culture, rewarding extraordinary performance where possible. In the military, where monetary rewards are not feasible, medals, citations, and superior-performance reports are used. In the commercial sector, the best performers are given preferential treatment for assignments and other incentives, sometimes monetary, unless represented by third parties and prohibited under work rules. The power of culture is immense.

Alignment is defined as movement in the same direction.[11] The vision and mission statements establish the direction of the organization. The alignment of the vision and mission statements is directly connected to the organizational culture. The ebb and flow of the vision and mission statements resonate throughout the company, as this is the basic and most profound revelation of the organization. The vision and mission statements are at the core of the organizational values, and when there is agreement between the vision and mission statements, there is fluidity throughout the organizational culture. The consonance is between the vision and mission statements, the leadership, and the employees of the organization.

Mission and Vision Alignment

Alignment with the vision statement is essential, but the mission statement can, and should, be functional for the strategic business unit. The mission statement is designed to keep the strategic business unit operational and competitive, with sufficient flexibility to consider emergent issues. Alignment with the vision statement allows greater divergence for the sake of the enterprise.

Small Consulting Firm Mission

In our previous example, the small consulting firm kept the mission statement very simple: "Work ourselves out of a job." The rationale of the owner was that if every contract allowed an opportunity to assist the client company in being independent in the specific area in the future, the client would be delighted as a result. All employees are schooled to take every opportunity to explain the services they are providing for the client, but they are also encouraged to take the time to explain the reasons for doing the tasks in that particular manner. The employees were also encouraged to incorporate client employees into the solutions for several reasons. When employees of the client organization are included in the solution, we realize three benefits: (a) the client organization has ownership of the derived solution, (b) the employees of the client are able to function independent of the consultant, and (c) the client organization would recognize greater value in the services delivered by the consultant. This approach translated into having a delighted customer who would encourage additional referrals, which was a good marketing approach.

Single Owner-Operator Mission

In the single owner-operator quilting business, there was no well-defined mission statement, but there was an operational definition that communicated added value for the customer. When it was necessary to articulate a mission statement, the single owner-operator would rely on statements such as "delivering good value" and "providing the customer their money's worth." In relation to the teaching component of the business, the idea was that there would be more quilts for the machine-quilting business. The machine quilting remained the mainstay of the business for several years. Teaching remained fun, but as the business matured, all activities were directed toward the generation of more business for the machine-quilting component.

Start-Up Consultancy Mission

The start-up consultancy used in our previous example has a mission statement that supports the vision statement, while allowing the focus to be on business operations, "Victory through every-day educational achievements." The owner of the start-up consultancy stated that "having dreams to become more than we are is key to future endeavors rising from the foundation of everyday achievements. Embracing dreams propels and forms the future of our lives. A single thought is enough to design a new future. The mission for future accomplishments denotes the outcomes. The hope for today is meeting all of the intricacies it takes to fulfill the vision in the long term. Victory everyday means celebrating the small and large accomplishments at every step. The intention is to keep the momentum of success moving while avoiding burnout." These thoughts can be qualified within the mission statement with clear communications. When mini-celebrations of accomplishments take place, there is internal validation and recognition of how rewarding the work has been, and the focus remains on accomplishments. The tendency is to emphasize victorious moments along the journey.

CHAPTER 6

Goals

The goals of an organization must be in alignment with its vision and mission statements, but the purpose of developing specific goals is to define the direction of the organization in more practical terms. Goals are established to be slightly out of reach but should be easily recognized by supervisory personnel and used for guidance in everyday operations. These goals would be positioned between the direction established by the chief and senior executive officers and that established by the managerial level. A good example of goals being in consonance with the vision and mission statements of the organization is The Coca-Cola Company press announcement of November 2009,[1] which stated,

> During today's session, the Company will discuss a number of key goals as part of its '2020 Vision and Roadmap for Winning Together' based on the "6 Core P's" of its vision:
>
> - Profit: More than double system revenue by 2020 while increasing system margins
> - People: Be a great place to work
> - Portfolio: More than double servings to over three billion a day by 2020 and be #1 in the nonalcoholic ready-to-drink business in every market and every category that is of value to us
> - Partners: Be the most preferred and trusted beverage partner
> - Planet: Be the global leader in sustainable water use and industry leadership in packaging, energy and climate protection
> - Productivity: Manage people, time and money for the greatest effectiveness.

Even more exciting is that the company's goals were apparently generated in collaboration with the bottlers and distributors rather than merely dictated by the parent corporation. This was reported in the November 2009 press announcement:

> "We worked with our bottling partners to create a 2020 Vision that is designed for action and guided by goals that will stretch us and enable us to continue to grow our business," said Muhtar Kent, chairman and chief executive officer, The Coca-Cola Company. "Working hand-in-hand with our great bottling partners, we are building a unified and aligned system equipped for long-term sustainable growth. With this roadmap as our guide, I am confident that we will usher in a new era of winning for the Coca-Cola system."

The element to note in this reporting is the inclusion of stakeholders in the decision-making process. This element of inclusion allows ownership of the goals in the resulting plan by all participants.

Goals Established by Executives

Executives are usually charged with developing the goals for their domains, or areas of responsibility, as a guide for the further development of the objectives by the employees. Essentially, these goals should be slightly out of reach and presented as something for all to strive for. If the goal can be attained in the near term, it would not be viable and would need to be modified to ensure continued effort to excel. Goals are established to encourage, motivate, allow professional and personal growth, and achieve excellence. It is within the domain of the executives within a strategic business unit to establish these goals in clear and easily understood language so that all employees can apply them as needed in the absence of specific guidance.

Set Goals High

Goals should be established to be slightly out of reach. Executives must be careful to balance their enthusiasm against reality. If the goals are too lofty, employees will not be motivated to reach a new, and higher, level of excellence. If the goals are set too low, the incentive for excellence is not present and any motivational opportunity is lost. The goals should be founded in reality and must be perceived to be achievable by all employees, yet they should still clearly communicate the need for more commitment.

Metrics Not Applicable

When the goals are set to be slightly out of reach, the use of metrics is inappropriate, and careful phrasing must be used in the formulation of the goals. If employees perceive that the goals are designed to be achieved, they may become frustrated, and productivity will decline as a result. However, metrics are not always excluded. It would be appropriate to establish a goal to increase sales by a certain percentage annually because it would present a viable target. The danger is that if sales for a given year exceeded that amount by midyear, the goal would have become an objective that was achieved, and employees would cease to devote attention to the pursuit of excellence. It would be far better to avoid the use of metrics altogether and allow them to be applied to objectives instead.

Goal Revision

When goals become reachable, it is incumbent on the executive to revise the goals to ensure that sufficient stimulation to excellence is retained. This can be accomplished in several ways, but the change must be visible and transparent to all employees, perhaps with some form of congratulations for achieving the goal. Employees should be rewarded for the accomplishment of difficult tasks that required a restatement of the established goals. The changing goals are a cause for celebration as an achievement by the employees.

Systems Approach to Alignment

The strength of the dynamic strategies concept is to develop and adjust strategy in a holistic process. When all system participants become owners of the process, the adjustments made necessary by changes in the operating environment become easier and more effective. In order to achieve this systems-level approach, all employees must understand how all elements of the strategic plan relate to one another. The employees should be involved in creating the portions of the plan that apply to their own areas of responsibility. When individual employees are involved in generating portions of the plan, synergy allows the formulation of an approach that (a) takes advantage of the intellectual capital[1] of the organization, (b) generates ownership on the part of each participant, and (c) creates an ability for the organization as a whole to respond quickly and effectively to changes in the operational environment.

The emphasis on goal setting rests on a holistic, or systems, approach that is in alignment with the vision statement, mission statement, and culture of the organization. In a traditional approach, the loops would be linear. Looping refers to the alignment of current processes to the direction established by predecessors. Any change in a predecessor process would necessitate a subsequent check for alignment. In Figure 6.1, the vision is established first and remains fixed over time. The mission is adjusted until it is in consonance with the vision and, in turn, will remain fixed until either the vision changes or the mission of the strategic business unit changes sufficiently to warrant a change in vision. The goals are tested against the mission and, if found in consonance, are tested against the vision. If there is misalignment, only the goals are subject to change. This is considered a linear approach, and it has been shown to be effective in a traditional environment.

The systems approach to goal setting must be in alignment with the vision established by the owner or chief executive officer (CEO) as well as with the organizational culture. When all employees are clear about

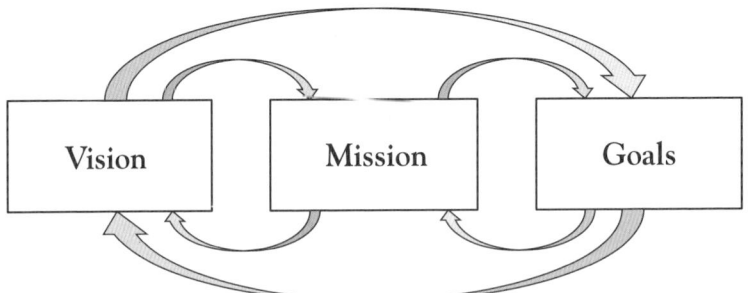

Figure 6.1. Traditional looping approach (© 2010 Seteroff & Campuzano).

the direction of the organization in both the near and long term, they are better able to assist in meeting the requirement of remaining highly competitive. In the traditional approach, the validation looping for alignment would ensure that the goals are in consonance with the vision, and when there is no alignment, the goals would be modified until there was consonance with both the mission and the vision. In the dynamic approach, the goals may become the driver in modifying the vision and mission. Alignment, however, remains the key element.

In organizations with several strategic business units, or with smaller organizations that operate in more than one arena, there will be a need to ensure that whatever strategic direction is taken, alignment with both the mission and vision is present. In the dynamic strategies approach, it would be permissible to address the issue holistically and modify the vision, mission, or goals as deemed appropriate by the needs of the operational environment.

Culture is the foundation of the organization and crucial to the dynamic strategies approach. Culture includes all stakeholders—it is not limited to employees. When we consider that organizations are composed of individuals working in concert to accomplish the vision, mission, goals, and objectives of the organization, it becomes paramount to ensure that all elements are part of the culture. In a well-established organization with empowered employees, it becomes very difficult to determine where individual culture and organizational culture meet.

The Small Consulting Firm

Continuing with the small consulting firm previously used as an example, the initial goals were the following:

1. Satisfy the client to build excellent references.
2. Make sufficient money to avoid working for someone else.

This seems to be typical of most start-up organizations, although the specifics may vary. Regardless of the vision and other theoretical considerations, the organization must remain operational and viable today in order to contemplate the future. In this specific case, two individuals who thought and practiced alike had no difficulty in satisfying the single client. There was no competition for their attention, and the client justifiably recognized that the organization was providing undivided attention. Because of the perceived excellent service, the client began to speak highly of the organization to others, and those firms began to seek their services. Meanwhile, the firm continued to deliver excellent service while seeking addition sources of business.

As the cash flow of the organization became adequate, a decision was made to continue providing excellent service. The organization expanded to include additional employees to take advantage of the new business being generated through referrals by existing clients. The goal was to retain a strong reputation. This was viewed as a critical juncture because the owner perceived that as more individuals were brought on board, control would have to be shared. The owner also realized that reliance on the integrity of the new employees was a risk factor. The goals were subsequently modified from the two original goals and expanded to four goals:

1. Continue to stress excellence in deliverables to the client.
2. Encourage all employees to generate their own work.
3. Generate sufficient revenue to facilitate bonus payments for excellence.
4. Bring new employees on board only if their values are in congruence.

Much of the goal setting was balanced by having the ability to say "no" to potential clients. Enhanced perception of quality resulted in the ability to charge a premium for services performed. This allowed a transition from the low-profit and delayed-payment clients into ventures that allowed delivery of services with a greater perception of excellence and greater respect for the quality of work by the client. Eventually the goals changed from the four revised goals to two simple statements, each with greater value:

1. Work ourselves out of a job.
2. Deliver excellence in everything we do.

The organization adopted a position that the reason the client hired them to perform services was because the client lacked the technical capability internally. If the organization took the approach of *working ourselves out of a job*, the perception of value by the client would be increased. Most formal contracts, and some informal agreements, included a caveat that the organization would work with employees of the client organization to generate appropriate solutions. This allowed the client organization to assist in developing the solutions and to take ownership of the resultant plan. When the client perceived the development of the plan to be internal, regardless of the guidance provided by the consulting firm, the client became committed to the success of the plan. As a result of this approach, successful implementations began to increase. It became abundantly clear that taking a position of encouraging members of the client organization to take the credit where it was deserved acted to enhance the perceived value of the services and resulted in additional business. These goals were sufficiently flexible to be unattainable in the short term and became self-motivating because of the lack of specificity.

The Single Owner-Operator

In the case of the single owner-operator quilting business, the initial goal was simply to recover the cost of purchasing a quilting machine and to receive discounts on fabric and batting for personal use. The quality of work quickly ensured that machine payments were being made on time, and when the machine was paid off, the goals were expanded to continue to obtain discounts on fabric and batting and to be able to make house payments. These goals remained in place for several years, and the preretirement goals were established:

1. Pay off the motor home.
2. Generate enough revenue to travel.

At the time of this narrative, the motor home was almost paid and the husband was looking forward to retirement in the following year. There is sufficient retirement income to support extensive travel in the motor home as well as some luxuries. The current plan is to continue working into retirement by taking on quilting assignments when not on the road with the motor home and to engage in teaching quilting to the maximum extent possible.

The Start-Up Consultancy

The first goal of the start-up consultancy business, previously used as an example, was to allow the owner to stop working at a nine-to-five job. The second goal was to provide an opportunity for individuals who desired to learn about themselves to experience spiritual growth in a safe environment. Individuals would have access to materials for self-discovery, and at the end of the course, would obtain the tools necessary to propel themselves forward in life. Simply stated, the goal was to get people from being "stuck" into a place where they could become "unstuck." On the professional level, the small consultancy firm assists professionals with self-discovery and provides tools to further careers. Leaders are fortified with cutting-edge tools to place them in a better position to assess, evaluate, change, and transform personal leadership styles.

At the organizational level, chief executive officers and leaders attend conferences where the leaders are trained to implement a spiritual business organization. These conferences review the model of a spiritual business organization as well as the implementation of the working tools. The working tools allow the leaders of their organizations to gauge the level of success the organization is experiencing and provide a metric for adjustment. The conference further develops networking and builds a system of support for the leaders. Finally, graduates may call the start-up consultancy business for follow-up support for a period of one year following the conference.

CHAPTER 7

Objectives and Strategies

Business objectives and the strategies used to achieve the tasks are the result of moving through the *Dynamic Strategies Model* from an enterprise vision statement, to a strategic business unit with a specific mission statement, to the goals designed to encourage and promote excellence. Objectives are the specific and measurable actions designed to address the established goals, or specific portions of the goals, in a predetermined sequence. These actions will advance the organization toward attaining its goals. Strategies are the detailed application of resources used to achieve the objectives.

Objectives Are Project Management (PM) Tasks

Objectives are clearly defined statements of work. When the objectives are accomplished, they will merge with other accomplished tasks to further attain the established goals. The objectives, or tasks, must be clearly defined and include the elements of a start time, a required completion time, and technical specifications that must be achieved. When possible, the accomplishment of the task should be assigned to a specific employee. Predecessors and successors should also be identified. The individual responsible for completing the task must be able to contact the employee responsible for the predecessor task to resolve any potential issues. The employee should also be able to contact the individual responsible for the successor task, or tasks, to communicate earlier availability or a delay in delivery. When a project manager is appointed, communication concerning successor and predecessor tasks would be accomplished through the project management office; however, having the specific predecessor and successor task information in hand allows for a personal touch on the task and allows the responsible employee the flexibility to be more productive through better communication.

Objectives Must Be Achievable

The objectives of the strategies used to achieve tasks are unique in that the tasks are not only achievable but also measurable. The strategies used to achieve the objectives become part of the detailed plan. Each task will have a specific start and a definite finish, with checkpoints clearly identified so that progress on the task can be measured. Each achievable task, when aggregated, results in furthering the goals established within the strategic business unit.

Start and Finish Dates

Each task should have a specific start time and a definite finish date so that the task may be placed in the proper sequence with other objectives. Start and end dates may be flexible, and as a result, the tasks may be scheduled to be performed at an optimum time, commensurate with the availability of resources.

Resource Consumption

Tasks are usually assigned to a single employee and will consume resources. The time that the employee spends on performing the task is also a cost in terms of resources. Materials consumed and the equipment needed to perform the task are additional expenditures of resources. The labor cost of supervision and other indirect costs are additional factors that should be included. Every task consumes resources, so the careful planning of the task, along with clear identification of the resources required to reduce the cost of doing business, becomes of paramount importance in the planning process.

Project Management Approach

The discipline of careful planning aligns well with a project management approach. The availability of project management software at a reasonable cost is an advantage. Inclusion of the project management discipline in most business education programs at the bachelors' and masters' levels allows the language of project management to be understood by most individuals in supervisory and managerial positions. Even in the smallest organizations, many leaders are graduates of formal education programs and have exposure to the discipline of project management. The terminology is easily understood and easily communicated to those without formal postsecondary education, so a common language is easily implemented. The language of project management should be uncomplicated, clear, precise, and easily learned and understood. The discipline of the approach is aimed directly at cost saving, and it has a great appeal for any organization.

Metrics

One of the benefits of the project management approach is the ability to establish and track the progress of each task. Part of the statement of work associated with each objective or task is a clear definition of how progress is to be determined at specified increments of time, at what cost, and to what specification. Each of these factors is determined during the planning process and is incorporated into a project plan that becomes available to all. Using a project management approach allows each of the established metrics to be tracked separately or collectively.

Time becomes a critical element because, in many organizations, labor is the highest cost of doing business. The manner in which time is used determines the cost. Tracking time becomes crucial for several reasons other than the cost of the task being monitored. The first factor under consideration is time needed to complete a task, with additional factors of direct and indirect costs. Finishing a task late will result in an inability to begin a successor task on time and may adversely affect the schedule. Finishing a task early may not seem to be a specific problem unless the early completion of a task results in an unacceptable gap in the allocation of resources. Careful attention must be given in order to achieve a balance of fixed and variable cost over time. This balance will assist in identifying an optimum mix of direct and indirect cost, resulting in the lowest total cost. This determination of optimum time—which carefully looks at the relative cost difference between fixed and variable costs to complete a task—takes place during the planning phase.

The discipline of "crashing"—which recognizes the tradeoff between fixed and variable costs—is unique to project management. In project management, each task along the critical path is "crashed" in turn until the point of minimum cost, or optimum project time, is achieved (Figure 7.1).

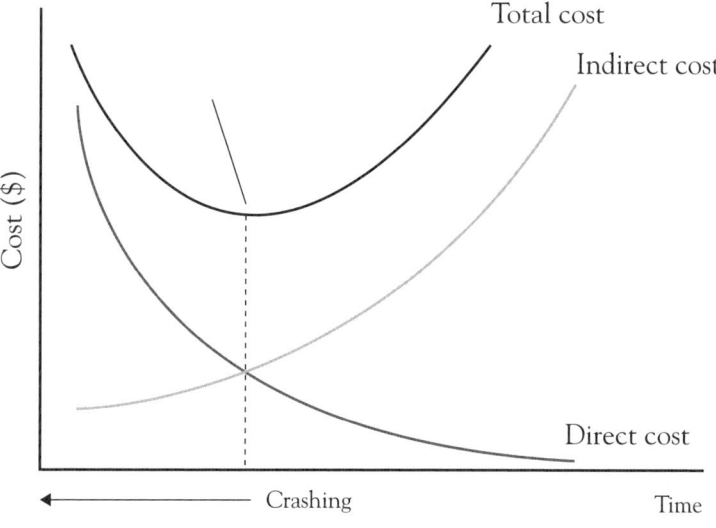

Figure 7.1. Project crash tradeoff (adapted from various sources).

Project managers will continue to "crash" a task until the cost begins to rise and then return to the optimum point. This will be repeated for each task along the critical path until the path shifts to a different path; this process is repeated until the entire project's minimal cost is known. External factors may not allow the use of the optimal project time, but as long as the optimum time for each task is known, the tasks can be tailored to meet the aggregate demands of the organization.

Cost Estimates

Using the crashing approach is but one element of determining costs. "Crashing" is a process that affects the manipulation of employee time in addition to other resources. All tasks consume resources, so the direct cost of materials must be included. Often omitted, but crucial to ensure the proper allocation of costs, is the cost of intangibles. Intangibles include the cost of facilities, equipment, and overhead costs of supervision with administrative costs. These costs are frequently rolled into a single percentage figure under the title of general and administrative expenses.

Determining the cost of doing business is largely an aggregate of the costs allotted to each task plus reserves for contingencies.

Most organizations have a preferred template that is used in determining the cost of performing routine tasks as well as one-time tasks. In larger organizations, the rules established by the accounting department, or by management, are used to establish intangible costs. The costing of the tasks is limited to performance measures and direct costs. In smaller organizations, rather than applying a formula, each task may be priced to meet the market. The reality is that the tasks must be performed to meet the objectives of the statement of work in such a manner as to meet the specifications of the customer while minimizing the consumption of resources. Anything short of acceptance by the customer is a failure.

Specifications

Technical specifications for the outcome of a task are essential to the dynamic planning process. Technical specifications are usually incorporated into the statement of work and become a part of the performance criteria. Having definite specifications is essential in ensuring that adequate performance objectives are met. There is some latitude in meeting specifications, but this is only possible in close coordination with the customer. In some cases, changing the specifications may be beneficial to both the organization and the customer, while at other times, the specification must be met as originally defined.

Technical specifications are generally contractual in nature but may be internally generated. Specifications may be engineered, established as an industry standard, or promulgated by government regulation. Many consumer goods, for example, must meet stringent standards for the composition of paint, size of the components, and in some cases, even the positioning of labels. These regulations may vary across national boundaries, and the organization must determine the best application of the regulations.

Some flexibility in specification is often desirable. For example, costs may be reduced by applying a more rigid specification for an off-the-shelf component rather than manufacturing a component to a lesser standard. The customer must always be consulted because the manufactured component may be specified at below standard because it is a sacrificial component designed to fail. The designed failure would serve to allow avoidance of a catastrophic failure of a more important component. However, if cost savings can be realized, it is incumbent on the organization to address the potential benefits to the customer so that all stakeholders may benefit.

Goal Accomplishment

Each of the measures of project management deals with the elements of success to include: time, budget, specification, acceptance by the customer, as well as alignment with goal accomplishment. Using the dynamic strategies approach, where all employees are aware of the goals of the organization and each employee strives to excel in order to achieve the goals in the most effective manner, creates an empowering environment. The mechanics of the dynamic strategies approach are augmented by a spiritual business organization. When the work environment is infused with spirituality, goal accomplishment becomes easier. In a spiritual business organization, performance and working with the intention of reaching the highest potential become a part of the employee's working nature. One premise of positive psychology states that a person will function at an optimum level that can be achieved by each individual.[1] This humanist aspect is further reinforced by a spiritual organizational culture because there is an increased sense of meaning and purpose to perform at an optimum level. The results are effective time management while performing with excellence.

Performance is increased with a spiritual business culture since there is a greater sense of economic performance. Economic performance in a spiritual business organization increases because there is a greater awareness of values, ethics, innovation, and productivity.[2] The organizational culture influences productivity.[3] A spiritual business organization does not have profitability as the main focus of the business, but as a result of a spiritual business organization, increased profitability is experienced. Garcia-Zamor stated that there is a 400% to 500% increase in profits over companies that do not incorporate a spiritual work place.[4] Many business leaders and professionals avoid the topic of spirituality in the mistaken belief that a spiritual business organization is primarily religious in nature and exclusionary in practice. In reality, a spiritual business organization may have religious overtones, but the essence is one of inclusion and acceptance rather than mere tolerance. Running a spiritual business organization may not be at the top of the list for most organizations, but as profits increase, performance rises, and employee retention is improved, spiritual business organizations are garnering more interest in corporate America.

A spiritual business organization is concerned with encouraging employees to reach the highest possible potential.[1] The focus is on promoting the individual to become more than can be imagined by the employee, with a humanistic approach of acceptance from leaders within the organization. The spiritualized leader encourages each individual to reach out and take advantage of education, personal development, and professional growth. There is an integration of personal and professional life that is freely expressed within the spiritual business organization. These elements become important, as each individual is influenced by the spirit and attitude of the leaders who promote a positive workplace. This workplace is filled with encouragement and is built on providing an organizational culture of acceptance where friendship, professionalism, mentorship, and even the concept of passion are included. These are the aspects of a successful spiritual business organization, where project management and empowered innovative techniques are encouraged. Once these elements are implemented and sustained over time, a progressive organizational culture allows the development of strategies that incorporate the diverse talents of all employees.

Strategies to Accomplish

Implementing the Dynamic Strategies Model requires an empowered work force, and it can be greatly assisted by a spiritual business organization that enjoys a high level of mutual trust under the guidance of spiritualized leaders. It is only when employees are allowed to act freely in applying the best techniques in a knowledgeable manner that the organization can enjoy the benefits in the form of reduced costs of doing business—and the result is an increase in profitability. When objectives are well designed and clearly defined, the resultant statement of work can be assigned as a task that allows flexibility in developing the strategy by employees at the most appropriate level, commensurate with the competency level of the individual.

Appropriate Level

Effective development of the strategies to accomplish tasks in an empowered organization is driven to the most appropriate level. Managers and supervisors must identify the individual best suited to perform the task and provide the support necessary for that individual to develop the strategies for accomplishing the tasks. This does not mean that there is no supervision, or that supervision is relaxed, but this technique shifts the supervisor from directing the work to assisting in coordinating the availability of resources to accomplish the tasks.

Employee Responsibility

The transfer of task responsibility is enhanced when the employee accepts ownership of the task through the detailed planning of the strategies associated with the performance of the task. When we change the role of the supervisor from that of a director to that of a coordinator, the responsibility for the success of a task can be successfully transferred to the employee. If the assignment is made with care, the employee to whom the task is assigned would be the employee with the most knowledge to accomplish the task. The employee would then be the best individual to determine how the tasks are to be performed, how to generate the strategies related to accomplish the tasks, and how to determine any contingencies that may be applicable. The supervisor, knowing the capabilities of the employee, would then be in a good position to coordinate the resources needed to accomplish the tasks.

The employee would receive the statement of work and technical specifications from the supervisor. After reading the statement of work and understanding the objectives, the employee would design the strategies needed to accomplish the task in detail. The detail would include estimates of time, resources, and performance metrics. The employee will have several tasks to plan in the course of the planning process, so a learning curve would be established, and each subsequent task would become easier. Once the planning process becomes an established part of the job, the employee begins to see the process as a routine aspect of the job. As employees learn to plan their own work, they will take responsibility for the outcomes associated with the application of the strategies. Since the employee developed the strategies for performing the task, the employee is in the best position to determine if a modification to the strategy is appropriate to improve task performance. Often, the immediate supervisor will assist in this determination.

The supervisor would be responsible for assisting the employee in the development of the strategies to accomplish the assigned tasks and in identifying the resources available. Since the supervisor would presumably be responsible for several concurrent tasks within the area of responsibility, he or she would be in a good position to determine available resources and to make assignments across these tasks. Being familiar with the technical aspects of each task, the supervisor would also be able to assist the employee in determining an appropriate modification to the strategies in response to emergent change from internal or external sources.

Estimated Time Frame

The employee and the supervisor are both in a unique position to estimate the time required to perform a task. The employee is often aware of the effective application of the tools and processes, which are not commonly known to those who do not perform the tasks on a routine basis. For example, there are often disconnects between engineered tasks and the field application of the process. In a personal communication with a heavy-engine mechanic for a railroad, it was clear that engineering specifications associated with assigned tasks are habitually overestimated. The time required to perform the tasks was overstated because many of the steps in a complex process could be performed in the shop, where the work progress is quicker, before being deployed to the field, where support equipment is not as readily available. In other cases, the engineered time estimates are underestimated because field conditions are not taken into consideration. Generally, the individual performing the task would be in the best position to estimate the time required. The difficulty in obtaining a viable time estimate for completion of the task would be largely based on the commitment of the employee to the success of the organization, the culture, and the level of spirituality.

In an empowered organization, the level of commitment is high. Employees are committed to the success of the organization, and the employee actively seeks ways to improve his or her own performance and offers suggestions to others, as appropriate. As employees gain trust in each other and collaborate actively in a culture that recognizes the value of the individual, enhanced performance results. There are many ways to estimate time, including the traditional project management computation of time estimate

$$TE = (a + 4m + b)/6,$$

where *a* is the optimistic time to accomplish a task, *m* is the estimated median time, and *b* is the pessimistic time.

The value of *m* would change based on the historical reliability of the individual providing the estimate. Although the traditional approach for estimating time is robust, the estimate is not developed by the employee, and so the responsibility for delivering the task within the specified time is not generally seen as important by the employee. When the employee actively participates in the development of the time estimate, and is included in the "crashing process" to determine the minimum possible time, the employee becomes committed to the success of the task within the estimated time frame. The supervisor plays a part in the process by ensuring that a viable time estimate is developed. The time estimate must be commensurate with the availability of resources, and it allows better understanding of how to allocate scarce resources effectively.

Estimated Resources

Resources are always scarce and often affect the ability to complete a task within the estimated time frames. Commitment of resources, or the promise of availability of the materials necessary to perform the task, is often questionable. An employee may be able to discretely identify the required resources to complete a task, but an employee usually cannot commit to the availability of the resources. Commitment of resources to accomplish tasks is usually controlled by the supervisors and managers in an organization. When supervisors are directly involved in determining the strategies to accomplish the tasks, a balance between time estimates and availability of resources can be achieved. Supervisors may be able to assist in distribution and use of resources that are unknown to the employee. The more knowledgeable the individuals are who are involved in the planning process, the closer the employees get to achieving a level of trust and collaboration. The collaboration positively affects the strategic planning to achieve the objectives.

Performance Metrics

As strategies are developed, time estimates are generated, and resource allocations are established, the employee and supervisor also develop performance metrics to ensure that the technical specifications are achieved. The overarching metric, as defined by the discipline of project management, is "on time, on budget, to specification, and acceptance by the customer." In an empowered organizational culture that enjoys spiritualized leadership, these traditional project management performance metrics are modified to "completion at a mutually acceptable time, under budget, to mutually agreed specifications, and to the delight of the customer." A mutually agreeable time is more effective because an ability to "crash" a task may arise due to several factors, including an unexpected event resulting from a lack of available resources, changes in process, or other unexpected factors. To be under budget is desirable because it should be the objective of every empowered employee in the organization to reduce the cost of doing business. Mutually agreeable specifications may become viable because advances in technology may offer an opportunity to improve the final product to the mutual benefit of all stakeholders. Finally, in marketing, a satisfied customer will return to do business with an organization in the future, but a delighted customer will tell others of their satisfaction and generate additional customers. Metrics, therefore, are an important component of the planning of strategies used to achieve the objectives.

CHAPTER 8

Metrics

Society expects performance to be at a defined standard, albeit variable among cultures, and organizations are no different. We measure the value of an employee to an organization by the quantity and quality of the work performed. For example, as children grow and develop, we measure their progress in height, weight, and other physical measures. As children begin school, we measure their proficiency in learning through examinations, and as adults, we measure every aspect of our lives against some standard. As more and more standards are accepted as the norm, we find that we cannot perform all the work society demands, so we become selective. Our work environments are no different. A typical job description, for even an entry-level position, provides so many variables that priorities must be established. Employees become very adept at determining which elements of the job description are actually being measured, and they concentrate on those metrics because they know that their overall job performance will be measured by the standards that their supervisor chooses to apply.

In an empowered organization, the perception of metrics undergoes a subtle shift. Employees begin to align their personal goals with the goals of the organization. As the employees start to see their performance in light of the success of the organization, they begin to understand that when they are pleased with their own accomplishments, the organization benefits. Spiritualized leaders understand that individuals are more critical of their own work, and they allow employees to establish their own metrics. Spiritualized leaders concentrate on providing the employee with opportunities for personal growth and professional development. The metric then transitions to the contribution that an employee makes to the overall objectives of the organization. Employees are therefore the ones who are best positioned to establish the metrics for implementation at a strategic level.

Applied at a Strategic Level

Applied strategies are a measurement of success that must be implemented at a working level. Supervisors and leaders in an organization must also perform to a standard established by the leaders themselves.[1] Any metric is based on the success of the employee performing the work. Employees may establish their own performance standards, but supervisors and leaders must be measured by the ability of the employees within their area of responsibility to achieve their aggregate standards. For this reason, the employee who seeks to satisfy their own performance needs, and who is the most critical of their own performance, is the measure of the organization.

Whatever performance metrics are established, the metrics must further the established goals and serve to accurately measure progress of the objective or the task. For tasks of short duration and low importance, a simple project management approach of started-task, work-in-progress, and completed-task metrics may suffice. For more sophisticated tasks with lengthy durations, progress reports may be required at regular intervals. Tasks along the critical path may require frequent progress reports so that appropriate interventions may be crafted to allow leaders to plan alternatives when necessary.

When metrics are developed at the objective or task level, and the metrics are incorporated into the strategies by the employee, the employee will view the reporting process as a part of the task. Employees sometimes see frequent reporting requirements as intrusive and counterproductive. When employees are involved in determining the balance between productivity and administrative requirements, the strategies to accomplish the task are better addressed, more adequately documented, and considered less onerous by the employee.

The employee who will perform the task knows the task best. Giving the employee the opportunity to develop the strategies to accomplish the task will result in the employee taking ownership for the satisfactory performance of the work. When we include the metrics to measure performance of the task in the planning process, we empower the employee to develop the strategies to accomplish the task and to provide the means to balance productivity and administrative reporting processes. Developing the metrics also serves to reinforce the ownership of the plan and to remove any doubt as to the performance criteria. A side benefit is that the employee will be clear about the performance and will be able to take early action to address any potential emergent issues that may threaten completion of the task on time, on budget, and to specification. In an ideal world, all employees would be self-motivated and empowered, with no supervision necessary. Reality would lead us to take more appropriate measures.

Employees feel more comfortable when they have a clear chain of authority, and leaders feel more comfortable when they can rely on supervisors to monitor performance. Supervision and coordination are important aspects of task performance. Supervisors are usually in a good position to evaluate the planning of the strategies to accomplish assigned tasks, and they must be involved in order to coordinate required resources. When metrics are developed by the employee, and agreed to by the supervisor, a feeling of trust begins to develop.[1] The supervisor becomes more aware of the capabilities of the employee to implement the strategies and to respond appropriately to changes in the operating environment that may affect the performance of the task. When the metrics are clear to both the employee and the supervisor, the employee becomes more trusting of the supervisor and can rely on the coordination of resources to accomplish the strategies. Periodic reports to leaders in the organization ensure that the tasks are being both monitored and accomplished.

Alignment

The alignment of tasks with the organizational direction is essential for success. Development of metrics at the task level is made easier when all employees in the organization are aware of the vision, mission, and goals affecting the tasks that they are involved with. Any metrics developed as a part of the strategies to meet the objectives must be in alignment with the goals. In larger organizations, the goals may be established by the project manager, working with the project sponsor, with a clear defined statement of work. In other situations, an executive may establish the goals for the various levels of an organization. In small business organizations, the goals could well be loosely defined by the owner. In any case, the more clear and concise the goals are, and the more effective the statement of work from which the objectives or tasks are defined, the easier it becomes to develop the strategies and the metrics.

Whatever the metrics established at the objectives and strategies level, the closer the alignment is with the goals, the better the metrics will support the vision and mission statements. When the metrics for each task are aligned, and in the presence of spiritualized leadership, the organizational culture supports empowerment. The spiritual business organization will achieve the ability to respond to change without sacrificing the ability to deliver at a mutually convenient time, under budget, to specification, and to the delight of the customer.

CHAPTER 9

Organizational Culture

Today, organizational cultures are influenced by multiple factors. Leaders have a concern for external and internal cultures that affect the success of the business. An acknowledgement of the differences between cultures is important since small businesses today have a global presence in one form or another. A lack of understanding of the customers of various cultures can potentially affect business profitability. A spiritual business organization is the competitive key for acceptance of cultural differences and, hence, an organizational culture that includes spirituality, which increases performance while maximizing profits.

External Elements

Acknowledging cultural differences becomes significant since a small or rather simple incorrect gesture can be offensive to the leaders or managers of an organization, at times resulting in the loss of a business partnership. Cultural differences are basic differences in the manner in which business is conducted, and that includes national mannerisms and behavior patterns. In the Middle East, it is an insult to sit with the bottom of your shoes showing, while in America, crossing your legs and showing off the name brand of your shoes is no cause for alarm. In Mexico, it is appropriate to greet one another with a kiss on the check, a hug, and a handshake, while in the United States, this same behavior might be viewed as sexual harassment. Understanding local customers becomes important since customs, even within the United States, are different from region to region. For example, a flowered shirt in Hawaii is appropriate business attire, while on the mainland in California, a suit and tie might be appropriate; however, a three-piece suit is almost essential in most business dealings in New York City or Washington, DC. Acknowledgment of cultural differences is important since profound issues may result from a lack of understanding such differences. External elements may appear to be external, but upon further investigation, all elements influence the organizational culture.

Cultural Intelligence

Cultural intelligence (CQ) is defined as the knowledge an individual possesses to function intelligently in diverse cultural settings.[1] Because business dealings have come to emerge on a global scale, cultural intelligence has become essential. This is the case even in small business. A small business may be located in a small town, but the suppliers of ink cartridges may very well be in China, while computer software is purchased from Europe, and so forth. The idea is simply to be knowledgeable of cultural differences in order to avoid making costly, irreparable mistakes.

Geographic Intelligence

The geographic intelligence (GC) of a culture extends to understanding how communication and language influence small-business decisions. Storytelling is an ancient form of communication that can be translated into today's use of metaphors. Geographic intelligence encompasses the knowledge that metaphors within a region may not cross geographical boundaries. Metaphors are used to convey concepts and clarify ideas; however, when the geographical area does not support the metaphor, effective communication does not occur. Leveraging knowledge of the geographical culture may assist in generating better-quality decisions. An understanding of when to use appropriate language across multiple cultures is called high behavioral intelligence within diverse cultures.[2] Using appropriate language and appropriate metaphors across cultures is important. That is not to say that a metaphor cannot work across regions, but the metaphor and the communication may need to be explained.

Local Culture

Considering the local culture of where the small business is located plays a role in communications within the organization, interaction with stakeholders, and the decision-making process. Using Southern California as an example, there are three very distinctive cultures. The local cultures are held within geographical areas: the desert, the mountains, and the beach. Generalities may be made in order to address the Southern California area, but at times, it is important to address specific cultures. The idea would be to have a culture of inclusion in order to achieve a level of success.

Ethnic Ambiance

Ethnic ambiance pertains to diverse ethnic-based cultures interacting with the small business organization. Throughout U.S. history, we have seen the struggles of different ethnic cultures. The roles of men and women vary greatly across all cultures, but we must be aware of the subtle differences that arise from ethnic differences. Other, more subtle differences may play a role in organizational decision making. The strategy would be to acknowledge all ethnic cultures while providing a service or product to benefit a diverse customer or client base.

Internal Elements

Internal cultures are complex and highly sophisticated. Constructive cultures[3] can be described as arising from cultural norms that promote motivation, achievement, self-actualization, individualism, and support a humanistic approach. Internal cultures provide the setting for motivation and self-actualization through the completion of tasks. Leaders provide an opportunity for additional education. Education enhances the opportunity for employees to experience professional and personal growth. Learning creates a working environment that fosters motivation[1] and leads to self-actualization.

The internal culture is generated by leaders' beliefs and example, while the employees create an internal culture where assumptions are understood through behavior at both the conscious and unconscious levels. Employees contribute to the cultural mix by moderating leadership behavior through a blend of several individual cultures. Internal cultures are dynamic and are in a constant state of change; however, the main theme of the aggregate internal culture remains dominant. Perhaps this can be clarified further by stating that the organizational culture is an amalgam of the several cultures that make up the organization.

Internal Strategic Business Units

Strategic business units may operate across local, regional, and even international boundaries. A single entity may find the need to have offices in several locations. When offices are staffed with several employees, the local culture of the office operates on the organizational culture to align the values of the local employees with those of the organization. Although the vision and mission statements, and perhaps the goals, remain the same as for other locations, the culture in each area may be markedly different. As long as the organizational culture remains sufficiently in consonance, the objectives may remain the same while the strategies may need to be tailored to achieve the required metrics. Leaders must be aware that differences in culture may modify the organizational culture within the same strategic business unit. Across strategic business units, the culture may differ considerably even though the units are located in the same general geographic area.

External Strategic Business Units

Due to the differences across strategic business units, leaders must be careful to allow employees to align organizational cultures to accommodate the values and beliefs of all employees, wherever dispersed. There is significant benefit to ensuring alignment across strategic business units because consonance increases productivity and satisfaction, reduces cost of operation, and decreases voluntary employee turnover. When strategic business units are aligned, the organization enjoys the benefit of moving employees for short-term assignments to fill emergent requirements, creating a more stable work force.

Individual Elements

Individual morals and values are not modified by the organization culture but may be subordinated or suspended in order to achieve security and acceptance. The danger with a mismatch of values or morals is that the level of satisfaction is lacking and the incidence of turnover is increased. Individuals join organizations but leave managers and leaders. When there is a disconnect between the values of the managers and the values of the employee, the employee will tend to become dissatisfied, productivity will decrease, and the propensity to leave the organization increases. Individual values take priority, and the employee will stay as long as the corporate values are not too unsettling. When organizational values become misaligned with individual values to an unacceptable degree, employees may tend to search for another job. It becomes increasingly difficult to stay within an environment that becomes toxic. At this point, job security and monetary compensation become less important than acquiring a sense of peace and a well-balanced life.

Family Inheritance

Individual values are grounded in family tradition. From our earliest consciousness, we begin to emulate our parents and extended family. As we approach entry into the school system, our values are essentially established. The values and morals of our playmates and adults comprising our new extended environment moderate these earlier values. As we mature, these changes become less significant. Family inheritance of morals and values appear to be a strong foundation for individual values in the workplace. Upholding family values, morals, and norms is one manner in which individuals continue their family legacy. Although these values and morals may be conscious or subconscious, family history remains the root of individual values, morals, and norms. Adhering to family inherited values provides a means of keeping family beliefs in a state of immortality.

Local Inheritance

Individuals are influenced by the locale in which they are raised. Local norms and customs drive behavior that affects individual and collective culture and morals. The local influence does not usually affect the familial culture but augments or reinforces inherited culture. The local culture often influences social behavior and contributes to the manners and interaction across gender and age barriers.

Peer Pressure

Peer pressure can be daunting since it starts from childhood and is carried into adulthood. Values are acquired throughout the continuum of life. The organizational culture promotes an environment that is reflective of the values and morals of the employees and the example set by the leaders. Individual values and morals are retained, but the application of these may change as organizational peer pressure increases. Peer pressure can be considered the enforcement of collective values and norms of the organization. The operational culture manifests itself as work behavior. Peer pressure may cause an employee to accept behavior of others that would not necessarily be accepted within the family because the majority of the group accepts the behavior. The employee is more willing to overlook the norm in order to gain a degree of acceptance within the group.

When the individual culture of an employee is not in consonance with the majority, issues of potential isolation arise. The employee who ignores peer pressure within the organizational culture is not accepted and is generally ostracized to some degree. Peer pressure, when acknowledged by the employee, will create a culture of inclusion or exclusion. A culture of exclusion may be detrimental to the organization, and when the leaders do not recognize this cultural dissonance, satisfaction declines and employee turnover increases. It is incumbent on leaders to foster and promote an organizational culture that is in alignment with the concept of a spiritual business organization.

CHAPTER 10

Spiritual Business Organization

A spiritual business organization[1] promotes the individual to the highest human potential within the organizational culture. The organizational culture endorses a safe environment for self-expression, individual and professional growth, and the development of others within the organization. A spiritual workplace entails a higher awareness that motivates employees to perform at a level of excellence.[2] A higher awareness comes from spiritual growth as an individual comes to an understanding that life is about self-discovery and leaving an imprint at work by performance.

The leaders of the organization set the tone for the organizational culture. The organizational culture is further developed through the directors and supervisors of the organization. The culture is fully expressed and experienced by the employees. It is imperative for the leadership to identify the informal leaders as the tone for the organizational culture is developed. The leadership of a spiritual business organization leads with heart. To lead with heart means to lead with compassion and cognition.[3] This type of leadership is characterized by a gentler approach to leadership, yet it obtains results because it is a culture with the foundations of respect, integrity, ethics, and honesty. This type of leadership is spiritualized leadership, and the leaders lead with the intention to empower employees to become more than what can be imagined. An essential element of this type of organization is clear and precise communication. Communication establishes a foundation of trust. When directions are clear, performance is not hindered by superfluous interference. Trust is built when the expectations are set forth in a manner that is precise and easily understood by the employee. Consistency promotes trust.

Organizations with a high sense of purpose create a spiritual workplace.[4] The organization[5] can then be further defined with a sense of meaning and purpose as it relates to the inclusion of a higher power, a deity, or God. God, as used here, refers to God in a religious sense and could be a Christian God, Islamic God, Jewish God, or God in another denomination. A deity is more generic in nature and a higher power is a more inclusive term. Small business provides meaning and purpose within the working environment by promoting employees to enrich their professional, as well as personal, lives. This is accomplished by instilling a set of values within the organizational culture. The leaders of the organization instill values by their behavior, and the employees have a tendency to mimic the leaders that they respect. In an outward expression of meaning and purpose, the leaders may choose to have a seminar to convey the organization's meaning and purpose. This type of "pep rally" is fruitful since leaders have the opportunity to convey the concepts in greater depth, and provide vision and mission statements, with the opportunity to demonstrate that the organization cares about its employees. This type of gesture does consume resources and temporarily reduces productivity, but it also returns more than is expended and may result in increased employee retention and satisfaction, avoiding the high cost of voluntary employee turnover.

The spiritual quotient includes mutual trust, respect, and responsibilities that become shared values. Trust is a value that assists in creating a safe working environment within the small business. When there is mutual trust within the organization, there is a flow of energy that results in a mutual understanding that situations, work, and events will be of benefit to the majority. Protecting the well-being of the employees as a whole, as well as advancing the business purpose, becomes the driving force of a spiritual business organization. Trust allows employees to work with confidence and a sense of self-efficacy, resulting in increased productivity and potential for greater profitability.

An ambiance of respect within the organizational culture makes the small business respect the clients and employees, communicating an image of a caring organization. A spiritual business organization chooses to be respectful no matter the circumstances. This respect is derived from the notion of a belief in a higher power, a deity, or God.

Sharing responsibilities benefits the entire organization so that the leaders and employees experience an increased quality of life at work.[6] When the leaders of the small business instill a culture of responsibility, the level of performance increases since there is an increase in self-efficacy. Nature denotes that a reasonable employee will embrace their personal responsibilities, and employees as a whole will be proud to perform at levels beyond the established acceptable standards. When employees embrace their responsibilities with pride, the culture is positively influenced. As more employees face their responsibilities with respect and pride and attempt to do their best, peer pressure begins to raise the bar for all employees, resulting in a culture that is constantly evolving for the benefit of the organization because it also meets the individual needs.

A spiritual employee is one who has a notion of God or a higher power to guide their everyday activities. A spiritual employee is more likely to make correct choices for the correct reasons, although this approach may vary with each individual employee.[7] A spiritual employee strives to leave a personal mark on the collective work, where group accomplishments are better due to their individual performances. The idea is one in which the spiritual employee is driven beyond their paycheck to perform at a level of excellence that surpasses expectations. The spiritual employee is driven by a relationship with God or a higher force, and if the organization supports this personal belief, the results are an ever-increasing level of trust and a culture of excellence. This level of motivation can be further emphasized within a spiritual business organization by leaders who not only encourage but also support and direct the efforts within the culture toward these beliefs.[8]

The competitive advantage of a spiritual business organization is profitability. Garcia-Zamor[9] acknowledged that organizations that support spirituality experienced a 400% to 500% increase in shareholder wealth, increased net earnings, and increased return on investments. This is the culmination of the spiritual values of designing an organization whose foundation is based on the notion of God or a higher power and thus exhibits the spiritual values of trust, honesty, and respect. These values are further amplified by exhibited behaviors that become part of the spiritual business organization. One element continues to link to the other, such as performance and doing one's best, in order to fulfill a personal spiritual need. As a result, there is excellent performance by employees.

A spiritual business organization is designed to include everyone within the organization and to promote the employees to reach their highest human potential. The organizational culture then fuels itself as the leadership and the employees evolve to become more, and the culture becomes inclusive.

Culture of Inclusion

A culture of inclusion is defined as bringing all parts of the organizational culture together by interacting across departmental lines, including leaders and employees. Although boundaries exist within the organization, these boundaries are connected to form bridges that include the culture as a whole. Pittinsky[10] referred to a similar concept as, "Weave cross-cut work-group roles with social-group membership in a systematic way."

A culture of inclusion strives to bring the organizational culture together, where all entities work with one another to promote the organization for greater success. The purpose of a culture of inclusion is to incorporate the whole company without divisions. The organizational culture is led by the leaders who promote teamwork. A single job is not locked into a box, but the culture of inclusion builds a friendly, helpful organization. If an employee needs help, others are ready to assist as necessary to move the task forward. The culture of inclusion does not take into consideration such concepts as "that is not my job description" or "I cannot perform that task" and instead focuses on customer service and how the job can be accomplished within the organization using the available resources.

A culture of inclusion entrenches itself by growing in customer service and in providing a unique experience where all employees are committed to the success of the organization. Employees appreciate their contribution to the success of the organization, especially when commitment is recognized with rewards. The organization then makes employees a part of the business as a whole, which then generates an ownership perspective. Starbucks[11] makes their employees partners and provides them with benefits, thereby creating a culture of inclusion. Simply put, a culture of inclusion involves the entire organization. Although individual jobs exist, it is the responsibility of all employees to serve the customer and to serve each other. The challenge is to design an organizational culture of inclusion for success.

Culture Is at the Root of Task Accomplishment

Culture is at the root of accomplishments, and performance may be considered an organizational element. Cultures are multifaceted and are composed of subcultures that influence thinking modalities and, more importantly, how things are accomplished.[12] Levine and Gottlieb[13] stated that tasks are accomplished by doing, and how things are completed is a distinguishing mark of the organizational culture. When the leadership promotes ownership of the organization to the employees, this generates a culture where performance is strong. Excellent performance then becomes an expectation of work, and employees are increasingly willing to perform to higher standards. Demands for higher performance might be viewed as a concept that generates stress and possibly increases employee anxiety; however, when the leaders are strong and able to communicate organizational goals clearly, change can then become a positive factor. Superior performance becomes the mechanism for accomplishing tasks.

The accomplishment of tasks becomes a part of the subcultures within the company, and the organizational culture in turn is fortified by the superior performance of the employees. An alignment with the mission and vision statements is an asset, as the culture is a reflection of the organization. A culture that has roots in accomplishing goals is supported when the proper tools are provided to the employees in order to accomplish tasks effectively and efficiently. Levels of frustration are reduced when all the tools necessary to accomplish the tasks work efficiently. This is an example of the need for a holistic approach in incorporating organizational culture as a foundation of the strategic planning process. However, the organization functions within an operational environment, and the cultures of all stakeholders must be considered.

External Business Influence on the Spiritual Business Organization

September 11, 2001, marked a turning point not only in the United States of America but on a global scale. As a result, the relationship between cause and effect became apparent to almost all employees. A sense of identification with others began to replace the single-minded approach to the workplace. As a sense of community expanded to include almost all aspects of life, a greater sense of spirituality developed in the workplace. A spiritual business organization attempts to return a sense of meaning and purpose within the work environment. The increased awareness of a global community allowed business organizations to adopt spirituality in the workplace, leading to increased competitive advantage on a global scale.

A spiritual business organization is influenced by external business and seeks a solution through encouraging its employees to meet higher standards. Spirituality is the new competitive advantage in business. Spirituality provides a deeper meaning and purposeful place for employees to work, thus decreasing employee turnover and increasing employee satisfaction and profitability.

Employees are looking to establish a balanced work life, where happiness includes spirituality.[14] The balance is one that includes personal, professional, educational, and social relationships. Although a balanced work life may not appear to be an external business influence, as business progresses, the leaders commence to understand the importance of a balanced life. The increased desire of employees includes spirituality at work, and this innovative concept gains momentum to propel individual productivity, and the business gains greater profitability.

Mixing and Matching to Become a Spiritual Business Organization

Leaders must recognize that there is a difference between spirituality and religion. There is also a distinction between tolerance and acceptance. In the workplace, the emphasis is on accepting the individual beliefs of each employee without condoning religious conversion practices. Most religions subscribe to similar values and beliefs, and where religious dogma differs, acceptance must be practiced.

As employees feel the freedom to practice their individual values in an environment of trust and acceptance, the organization benefits through increased job satisfaction and productivity. Since honesty and integrity are the keys to most applied values, a higher moral standard will lead to fewer administrative interventions and reduced litigation. Leaders who create this safe working environment should reap the benefits of a spiritual business organization through a reduction in the cost of doing business.

A successful spiritual business organization mixes and matches spirituality. The concept is not one of tolerance but one of acceptance of each employee's beliefs. The idea is to accommodate the employee with their beliefs in an environment that is supportive and nonthreatening. When the spiritual business organization supports a spiritual system by providing an ambiance where the notion of God or a higher force is accepted, then the barriers are removed and the employee is empowered. "Mixing and matching" refers to a spiritual business organization accepting spirituality, and not necessarily a particular religious belief, to be part of the organizational culture. When empowerment is present in a spiritual business organization, the result is greater productivity, increased satisfaction, and reduced turnover. In this context, the cost of business is reduced and there is increased profitability in a highly competitive global operating environment.

CHAPTER 11

Model Sensitivity

Model sensitivity is the ability of the model to respond to changes in the operating environment. Models must be flexible enough to respond to change within the scope of the operations. The parameters of applicability determine the usefulness of the model. The dynamic model, when implemented in a spiritual business organization with spiritualized leadership, is applicable to small business organizations and is sensitive to rapid changes in the operating environment. The Dynamic Strategies Model has limitations. The larger the organization, and the more hierarchical the organizational structure, the less sensitive the Dynamic Strategies Model becomes and the more effective the traditional strategic planning approach becomes.

Zero-Based Approach Not Essential

A zero-based approach assumes that all known information is suspect, and each element must be researched and supported. This is a costly and time-consuming exercise. Implementation of the Dynamic Strategies Model is cost-effective in small organizations with hands-on leaders and empowered employees because the operating environment is well known to all stakeholders. Since the focus is narrow, the individuals involved are generally well versed in the operational conditions. The internal knowledge is frequently augmented by membership in one or more industry-related or professional societies. Society membership frequently allows access to industry-specific analysis and marketing data, along with providing technical conferences and networking opportunities. The need for a true zero-based approach is seldom essential even though it may be highly desirable. The dynamic strategies approach allows the use of current and well-understood information to create an appropriate response to changes in the operating environment without extensive research.

Addressing Change

Change is driven by both internal and external factors. The senior leaders of the organization prepare the foundational change information well in advance. The difficulty arises because—unless the leaders are involved in the hands-on operations on a daily basis, such as in a small organization—a separation between the work performance level and the senior leadership begins to emerge. The greater the distance, or levels, between the decision-making leader and the employee performing the work, the greater the potential that change will be addressed inappropriately. The Dynamic Strategies Model is scalable, but it works best when applied in a small, flexible, and spiritual business organization. All organizations are change-driven, and all organizations need to respond appropriately and quickly to change. The Dynamic Strategies Model allows the response to change to be applied at the most appropriate level of the organization, commensurate with the comfort level of the leaders.

Lowest-Level Decisions

Change is a constant in the operating environment of any business organization. The velocity of the change determines how leaders view the urgency of an appropriate response. Determining the level at which the decision is made becomes a crucial factor. In a very small organization of one or two individuals, the response to change is usually a matter of who recognizes the need to change first. In larger organizations, rules may dictate the level at which the decisions are made in order to respond to changes identified at a lower level. When the response is at a higher level than the one where the need for change was detected, then delays due to clarity and timeliness of communication will usually become a factor. For example, an employee recognizing that a procedure is inappropriate, but who does not have the power to effect a change, may communicate the need for a change but may be constrained by the process instructions to continue performing the task as directed. During the decision-making period, the work being performed may range from a minor inconvenience to a total waste of time and resources. The decision-making process may be compounded by imperfect communication of the underlying issues, and, consequently, the response may be inadequate. For these reasons, the most effective responses to emerging change in the operating environment are made at the level closest to the performance of work.

Employee Abilities

Not all employees are created equal. Some employees possess greater skill levels in their assigned roles. Some employees have better preparation and training, and some employees have more experience than others do. Some employees, by their on-the-job performance, have earned the trust of their supervisors and often enjoy the respect of their peers. Many of these high performers will also take pride in their work. These employees will not only make an effort to maintain their current skills; they will also seek to improve their skills and knowledge through engaging in outside education and training activities. These employees are a good source of information, and they are generally more flexible in responding to change because they are open to observing the operating environment to a greater degree than many of their counterparts in similar roles. These highly skilled employees may become the drivers of change within the organization. These employees network with other similarly skilled individuals and become aware of the changes taking place in other organizations. The Dynamic Strategies Model allows the changes to be applied to the organization and driven from the bottom up.

Other employees may find themselves in pursuit of lifelong learning, and they not only enhance their skills and knowledge within the discipline of their employment but also seek to expand their knowledge further. These individuals move through lifelong learning and expand their networks across a broad range of individuals. Some individuals will be from outside their trade or discipline, offering an opportunity for cross-pollination of ideas, which may result in unexpected opportunities for improving performance. These lifelong learners are constantly striving to apply the new information they are obtaining in meaningful ways, and the organization can benefit from their dedication to learning. In a spiritual business organization, the increased level of acceptance allows the employee to assist by contributing both within and outside the confines of the job description. It is then incumbent on the leaders to remain open to the possibility of change being driven from sources other than the traditional top-down or bottom-up scenarios. Lateral or diagonal drivers become a possibility.

Social involvement may also provide knowledge that is unexpected in the normal course of employment. Many employees participate as volunteers in social and service organizations or perform other volunteer tasks in their community. In the performance of their volunteer work, or through their social engagements, the employees become exposed to information that could be used to enhance their own position within the organization. Employees could potentially provide information that can assist in preparing the organization for change in a timely fashion. Today, with information being so crucial in the conduct of business, many spiritualized leaders are learning that it is to the benefit of the organization to encourage their employees to actively participate in the community. Spiritualized leaders frequently offer substantial support by committing resources as part of an effort to project corporate social responsibility.[1] Public relations efforts that highlight the employee and that also identify the organization as being socially responsible can lead to greater visibility and reduction in the cost of doing business, as well as expose the employee to information pertaining to change in the operating environment.

A spiritual business organization, with a culture of inclusion and acceptance[2] and when led by spiritualized leaders, creates an organizational culture in which employees thrive. When the employees are satisfied and become committed to the organization, the opportunity for collection of information by scanning the external environment becomes enhanced. When employees become empowered and well informed, they are able to drive needed change in any direction with confidence. When employees are empowered to makes changes within the operational parameters, their performance will be noted and their actions rewarded.

Organizational Parameters

An organization is driven by formal and informal information, gathered from internal and external sources, allowing it to function within established parameters. Not all information is relevant, and the organization does not necessarily wish to be driven by market forces into areas in which the organization does not wish to participate. The boundaries, or parameters, are established by the vision statement, mission statement, and, to a lesser extent, the goals of the organization. When all employees are aware of the parameters, the suggestions for change are more focused and more appropriate to the tasks. Some organizations actively encourage the collection of information by their employees, and when outside the parameters of their own organization, the leaders exchange the information with stakeholders for mutual benefit. The key element is to make the employees aware of the boundaries within which the organization operates. When employees are aware of these parameters, contribution to the success of the organization is more focused and relevant.

Bottom-Up Potential

When leaders recognize and encourage the growth potential in employees, the ability for the employee closest to the work at hand is able to determine an opportunity quickly. In the context of the bottom-up approach to problem solving, where the solution is closest to the point of recognition, employees enjoy the benefits of (a) earlier detection of the need for change, (b) greater knowledge of the elements requiring change, (c) a clear perspective of alternative solutions, and (d) quicker implementation of a solution. In a spiritual business organization with empowered employees, this problem-solving ability is enhanced.

Employees familiar with their discipline beyond the usual scope of their assigned tasks can be valuable in detecting inappropriate or ineffective strategies. Spiritualized leaders create an environment of mutual respect and trust. When employees take advantage of learning opportunities, the ability to detect a need for change—and more importantly, the ability to recognize the elements requiring change—becomes a clear advantage to the organization.

Not all strategies associated with the completion of an objective or task may need to be changed in order to realize improved performance. Frequently, a small adjustment in one or two elements of a strategy can result in significant savings in time and physical resources. When leaders and employees have the ability to recognize the elements that contribute the most to achieving the strategies with the least disruption, this becomes a situation well worth developing.

The ability of leaders and employees to discern the most effective adjustment to strategies is a matter of perspective, and it is best practiced in a culture of mutual respect and trust. The perspective of the employee performing the task may differ greatly from the leader that observes the operation. The further the leader is separated from the task, the easier the task appears. The leader observing the task is probably not aware of the skills necessary to perform the task. When leaders recognize that the employee performing the task understands the task best, then the employee recognizes that the work assignment is recognition of their ability to perform. With increased trust and respect, the employee begins to look for ways to improve his or her individual performance and the defined process. When leaders fail to listen, and when leaders do not allow change to take place, administrative costs increase.

The advantage of the bottom-up potential in the Dynamic Strategies Model is the ability to reduce the cost of doing business. The Dynamic Strategies Model allows competent employees to initiate change at the time a need is recognized. Not all changes will be beneficial, but each change contributes to the lessons learned by the leaders and employees in the organization. When positive outcomes are recognized and rewarded, trust emerges. No organization can exist for long with a high rate of poor decisions, but each decision, whether good or poor, is an opportunity to learn. Poor decisions are easy to recognize because they are very visible. It is more difficult to look carefully at a good decision to determine if it could have been performed better.[3] In each case, the objective is to determine if the response time could have been better, which should lead to better awareness in future opportunities.

Systems Approach

This dynamic strategies approach is about using human capital[4] effectively. Developing an organization where individuals are treated with trust and respect, and where an atmosphere of acceptance prevails, results in a spiritual business organization.[5] Increased employee satisfaction and improved financial performance is the result of developing a firm where trust and respect are a part of the organizational culture.[6] For all practical purposes, the organization has little or no control over the price of its product in a free-market economy. Leaders must concentrate on reducing costs. Fundamental economic principles provide a standard formula, as follows:

$$\text{Profit} = \text{Total Revenue} - \text{Total Cost}$$

$$(\pi = \text{TR} - \text{TC}).$$

If we further accept that

$$\text{Total Revenue} = \text{Price of the good or service} \times \text{Quantity}$$

$$(\text{TR} = \text{P} \times \text{Q}),$$

organizations must significantly differentiate themselves from other companies and their products in order to compete in a saturated market where most small businesses operate. The market establishes the price, so the volume of business determines the revenue that will be generated by the business.

Total cost has long been the domain of management and has resulted in a multitude of approaches. In an economic downturn, it is not unusual to see an economic spiral where employees are laid off, and there is a reduction in purchasing power. Reduction in purchasing power results in layoffs in supporting sectors, contributing to the downward spiral. Few small business organizations possess the resources to sustain operations for an extended period without a strong revenue flow. The drive is to continuously reduce the cost of doing business. This is usually accomplished by cutting overhead and eliminating, or consolidating, middle-management positions and having higher-level executives take on a greater role. In some "flat" organizations, there are few overhead positions. In this respect, the flat organizations begin to resemble the small business organization.

In a small business organization, a systems approach[7] is very visible. Leaders recognize the organization is based on the skills and dedication of their employees and that they must constantly learn to stay competitive. Leaders in small business must perform many diverse functions, but the successful leaders concentrate their efforts on ensuring the formation of a learning organization.[8] To ensure a viable learning organization,[9] leaders must practice a systems approach that makes use of every opportunity to design an organization of respect and mutual trust. In a spiritual business organization, where employee satisfaction is a constant, the organizational culture is one of empowerment. The Dynamic Strategies Model supports the concept of people being the most important element of the organization.

Environmental Scanning

The purpose of environmental scanning is to seek opportunities for change in order to improve performance and increase profitability. The Dynamic Strategies Model is sensitive to change, but change can be proactive or reactive. Reactive change results when changes come as a surprise, and this often causes stress by requiring prompt action. Proactive change is less stressful on the organization but requires constant scanning—that is, actively looking for change in both the internal and external environments. Any change in the operating environment requires an evaluation, followed by a decision to respond to the stimulus of the change, to ignore the change, or to defer action on the change. When the change comes unexpectedly, the time available to engage in the analysis is usually short, but the Dynamic Strategies Model is sensitive to the decision-making process by allowing empowered employees to design a response without a lengthy communications process.[10] In a proactive approach, where change is anticipated, the empowered employee can incorporate the change within the area of practice or competence in a measured manner with little personal risk.

External Environment

Changes resulting from an environmental scanning process and requiring action are typically driven by external factors. External factors may consist of changes in the industry, changes in the market, emergent technology, or a myriad of other factors. External environmental scanning includes the reading of trade and professional journals; membership in civic, service, and professional organizations and societies; and staying in touch with political and economic information. Changes resulting from internal factors can usually be planned more carefully, unless a situation arises in which a competitive advantage can be gained. When a competitive advantage can be obtained, the internally driven change may take on some urgency.

Employee Responsibility

All employees, from the chief executive officer to the newest employee, should be responsible for developing the information necessary to determine the need for change. It is impossible for a single individual, at whatever level in the organization, to be aware of all external and internal factors. Information must be collected, and it must be shared.[11] Information collection can only be effective when every employee is intimately familiar with the vision and mission statements and when employees understand the goals of the organization. Well-led organizations invest in affiliations with selected organizations and societies and encourage their employees to participate. Affiliations with professional and industry organizations allow leveraging of the network potential to obtain emergent information in a timely manner to adjust organizational goals. Increased opportunity for networking may lead some employees to seek alternative employment, but a spiritual business organization, under spiritualized leadership, provides an atmosphere of employee satisfaction and trust so that voluntary employee turnover[12] is minimized. When all employees are alert to changes in the external environment, a proactive approach to change benefits the organization. Free exchange of information allows the Dynamic Strategies Model to guide the response to the change at the most appropriate level.

Industry Boundaries

Change can be applied across the industry, and membership in industry organizations and professional societies can provide the earliest information on the characteristics of the change. Membership can also disclose the actions others may have taken. Incorporating industry information can be beneficial because it provides a pattern for both successful and failed responses. All organizations should learn from both success and failure.[13] Margaret Wheatley, in her *Lessons From the New Workplace,* stated that after every important event, we should ask what happened, why do we think it happened, and what can we learn from it? To this should be added, how do we implement the lesson? Or, where do we go from here? Any information from reliable sources may be of value, but until converted into an action plan, the information has little value and simply consumes resources. To be of value to the organization, all information from industry sources or personal contact should be viewed through the lens of the Dynamic Strategies Model.

The problem with information is that it must be placed into the proper context before an action can be taken to respond to the change. The reflexive thinking[14] process is assisted by awareness of the vision statement, mission statement, and goals of the organization. Many employees pride themselves on being experts in their field of endeavor.

The research skills model, shown in Figure 11.1, responds to the proliferation of experience-based hiring practices. This human resources practice has encouraged hiring based on training and previous experience, while minimizing general knowledge as a hiring factor. This human-resource-based process ensures that new hires are quickly productive. This practice must ensure continued profitability of the organization. Care should be taken to provide a balance between knowledge and experience, with an ability to perform research as the discriminator. The research can be academic or merely an awareness that there are many factors contributing to the success of an organization. Each employee should contribute to the success of the organization to be competitive and remain viable. Scanning the industry and the external environment is essential.

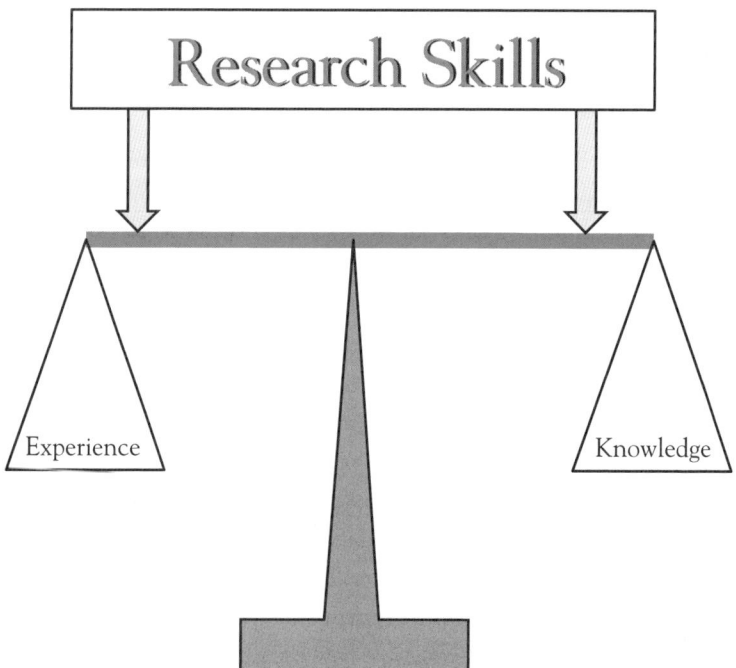

Figure 11.1. Research skills are important to provide balance (© 2010 Seteroff & Campuzano).

Organizations concentrate their hiring efforts on either experience or knowledge. As a general rule, entry-level positions concentrate more on knowledge in the form of education, degrees, or certifications. Experience and certifications play a larger part in the hiring process for more senior positions. Once hired, many business organizations encourage their employees to seek additional certifications or higher educational degrees. In the application of the Dynamic Strategies Model, a spiritual business organization creates a learning organization that applies formal and informal research. Reflexive thinking generates creative solutions to emergent changes. The difference is that reflexive thinking can, and does, take place at the most appropriate level in the organization. It is this ability to perform research to ensure better-quality decisions that sets the spiritual business organization apart from the competition.

SWOT Analysis

The traditional analysis of strengths, weaknesses, opportunity, and threats (SWOT) is widely used in a strategic planning process. The information for a SWOT analysis comes from multiple sources, both internal and external. The SWOT analysis has many derivatives, but the fundamental tool of analysis remains unchanged. Information is first sorted into external or internal categories, with strengths or weaknesses both being internal in nature, while opportunities and threats are external. Each element of new information from an external source is evaluated on the basis of whether it poses a threat or presents an opportunity. The next step is to determine if the internal organization is strong enough to respond to the threat or to take advantage of the opportunity. Although this approach is highly respected across many industries, it does not address the uncertainty[15] of the actions resulting from the analysis. Many other tools of analysis are available and should be used if the expertise of the employees permits; however, SWOT analysis is easily understood and fits well into the decision-making process within the Dynamic Strategies Model.

Leaders using tools of analysis, including SWOT analysis, determine the need for change. Employees, when empowered and functioning within a spiritual business organization, can also apply the tools of analysis, formally or informally, to implement needed changes. When employees are involved in scanning the external environment—and when they consider the vision statement, mission statement, and goals of the organization—communicating their observations to the leaders is appropriate.

Employee Communication

Employees must know how to communicate information regarding change and know who needs the information. Traditionally, all decisions were made at the leadership or management levels, and the changes were communicated downward. When employees are empowered, they make the decisions at the most appropriate level. A communication issue arises when an employee has information pertaining to a change that does not affect the work the employee participates in. At this point, it is important that the employee knows who needs the information and knows how to communicate this information in a brief, clear, and concise manner. When an organization has transparency and employees are aware of the work in progress, the organization benefits in two distinct areas. First, the employee can perform their own assigned task better when they are aware of how their task fits into the scheme used to address goals. Second, the employee is aware of who else can use the information. The method of communication can be formal or informal, documented or undocumented, or specific or general. Spiritualized leaders must establish the means for both communicating the overall strategy to each employee in an appropriate manner and establishing a framework of communications that will foster the exchange of information.

Change in Multiple Areas

Leaders and supervisors play a significant role in the exchange of information. Employees may obtain information that they cannot apply within the framework of their own responsibility, but they may believe the information would benefit the organization. Alternately, the employee may see an opportunity for collaboration to enhance the tasks to which the employees are committed. In either case, the employee can relay the information to their supervisor and to another employee who they believe would benefit from the newly acquired information. The supervisor allows better coordination of available resources and offers an opportunity to collaborate on a response to change. In an internal environment where trust and respect is present, an effective exchange of information can be supported. The Dynamic Strategies Model allows employees, supervisors, and leaders to collaborate as necessary to achieve the best possible results with the available information.

Internal Environment

The internal operating environment is made up of many factors. Culture plays an essential role in defining the internal environment, and it is the foundation of the Dynamic Strategies Model. The chief executive who determines the direction of the organization by creating the vision statement must carefully consider the existing culture or change the culture to accept the vision. Leaders of strategic business units should take culture into consideration in preparing a mission statement. Executives who determine the goals of the organization should consider the organizational culture to ensure the goals are acceptable by the employees. Employees should become familiar with the tools of analysis, and the metrics established must be cost-effective and appropriate.

Tools of Analysis

Many tools of analysis are available to assist employees in the decision-making process. No tool is specifically recommended, and no tool is excluded, in the use of the Dynamic Strategies Model. The traditional tools of strategic planning are effective and, if cost-effective, should be used. Tools and processes that are familiar to the employees making the decisions are appropriate. A viable spiritual business organization that invests in the training of all employees reaps the benefits by having the employees make better-quality decisions by using more sophisticated analytical tools. The concern would be to avoid extensive analysis to arrive at a decision. Care should be taken to ensure that the cost of analysis does not exceed the cost benefit of implementing the response.

Financial Tools of Analysis

Financial tools are usually appropriate because they are easy to track. Any scheme should be devised to be both cost-effective and appropriate. As a minimum, financial tools are used to track the effectiveness of strategies in accomplishing the objectives or tasks. Standard project management tools to track performance provide a solid guideline because these tools can be quickly developed from routine reports and, depending on the aggregation, can provide leaders with a multilevel perspective.

Cost variance (CV) is a common measure, and it is composed of a comparison between the budgeted or planned cost of work performed and the actual cost of work performed, as represented in the following equation:

$$CV = BCWP - ACWP.$$

For short-term tasks, this measure is included in a completion report. For a longer-duration task, where progress is reported at specified intervals, cost variance has the benefit of looking at the effectiveness of the planning process as well as the expenditure of resources on performance of the task. Shorter tasks do not allow the application of the Dynamic Strategies Model because of the insufficient time available to respond to change.

Schedule variance (SV) is also a common measure in longer-duration tasks. Schedule variance is a difference between the budgeted or planned cost of the work performed and the scheduled cost of work performed, as shown by the following equation:

$$SV = BCWP - SCWP.$$

The scheduled variance metric is also not suitable for shorter duration tasks because there is insufficient time to respond. For longer duration tasks with several reporting periods, the metric is effective in establishing a trend. The trend allows leaders to determine a need for change and to determine an appropriate response.

Cost variance percentage (CV%) is often used because it provides a percentage instead of a dollar amount. The cost variance percentage allows a comparison of progress on several tasks of unequal dollar value. The cost variance percentage appeals to leaders who wish to compare relative effectiveness in the implementation of strategies to achieve objectives. The cost variance percentage is a result of dividing the cost variance by the budgeted cost of work performed:

$$CV\% = CV/BCWP.$$

Other financial measures are appropriate, and each organization has their favorite methods. The emphasis in this section is on providing some examples of metrics that may be applied at the objective or task level. Organizations should ensure that any financial metric that is applied does not cost more than the value it brings to the implementation of the plan. Labor is expensive, and the costs of collecting data are significant. Where possible, financial data should be collected as a part of task performance. The application of metrics at the task level would be available to all employees involved in the performance of the task as well as to supervisors. When applied consistently, and early, a need for change in the process may be observed quickly, and the employee can apply an appropriate response.

Productivity Measures

Productivity measures must also be cost effective, and appropriate, to ensure that the cost of data collection does not exceed the savings from the application of the collected data. Productivity measures are elusive. Leaders can underestimate the complexity of the tasks, and employees may recognize that their performance could be improved. The reality is that any measure of individual productive is arbitrary and faulted. Organizations use productivity measures that sometimes appear arbitrary to the employees. In a spiritual business organization, with a high level of respect and trust, the burden is eased by the application of the Dynamic Strategies Model at all levels of the organization. There are two project management specific productivity metrics that can be applied at a reasonable cost to the organization because the raw data are a normal part of conducting business. The two project management metrics are earned value (EV) and schedule variance percentage (SV%).

Earned value (EV) can be determined by comparing schedule and cost. As in the following formula, the schedule factor is derived from dividing actual progress (AP) by scheduled progress (SP), and the cost factor is derived by dividing the actual cost (AC) into the budget cost (BC):

$$EV = (AP/SP) / (BC/AC).$$

Schedule progress is usually determined by the supervisor or the employee performing the work, while cost is derived from the financial data.

Schedule variance percentage (SV%) is another composite approach that returns a percentage. The percentage is generally preferred by managers and leaders as a measure of productivity because of the ability to compare tasks with varying dollar values. The schedule variance percentage is derived by dividing the budgeted cost of work scheduled into schedule variance:

$$SV\% = SV / BCWS.$$

There are other ways to measure productivity, at both the individual and collective levels, and each organization will choose the method that is the best suited. The two metrics provided here are typically project-management-based and are usually reliable.

Organizational Structure

Organizations can be structured in many forms, from a very formal and traditional hierarchical structure to a very informal organization. Many large organizations are now attempting to revert to a small-business structure, often using a team approach, to achieve the flexibility of small business organizations. Small business organizations are usually less formal and more flexible, at least initially. As small organizations become more successful, the trappings of structure begin to emerge. When small organizations begin to grow, the added layers of administration add to overhead costs.

Formal Organizational Structures

Formal organizational structures have the advantage of a clear and well-defined chain of command and responsibility. In a true hierarchical organization, there are several layers of management, and the information flow is upward in the chain of command. The decisions are made at higher levels and the resultant flow is downward. The Dynamic Strategies

Model supports a downward decision flow-well, and, for this reason, the Dynamic Strategies Model is presumed to be scalable.

Low Overhead Requirements

An organization must achieve the lowest possible overhead costs to be effective. Any level other than the one at which the work is performed is overhead. Large and medium-sized organizations have worked diligently to flatten their organizations by removing unnecessary layers of supervision and management. Flattening the organizations is an effort to reduce the cost of doing business. Increased automation and providing reporting tools to employees who perform the work allows for fewer levels of supervision and management while allowing leaders in the organization to make decisions based on solid information.

Small business is not immune to the need to cut operating costs. Small businesses responded to the 2008 economic downturn in the United States by incorporating creative measures. Over a quarter of small business organizations have reduced their facilities costs by encouraging employees to work from home.[16] Most small business organizations tend to reduce the services they use or services they provide to their employees. Even organizations that are affected by economic downturns to a lesser degree are forced into a cost-cutting mode of operation in order to stay competitive in a market that rewards organizations of whatever size that reduce costs.

Flexibility

Organizations of any size should be flexible to allow changes to be implemented quickly and at the most appropriate level. The Dynamic Strategies Model allows for a quick response to change. Larger organizations could also benefit from using the Dynamic Strategies Model to the extent that the leaders are able to implement the model within their existing organizational structure.

Informal Organizations

Informal organizational cultures develop when employees perceive the formal organizational structure to be ineffective. Informal structures also materialize to meet social needs of the individuals. When employees perceive that the organization is not meeting their needs to be productive, the employees will begin to develop informal channels of communication. Additional channels of communication develop when like-minded individuals gather in the same location. Employees quickly find out who goes to the same church, belongs to the same organizations, and whose children participate in similar activities.

Informal organizations foster and promote tolerance, and in a spiritual business organization, acceptance is the norm. The Dynamic Strategies Model accommodates the formal, as well as the informal, organizational structure by allowing decisions to be made at the appropriate level within the organization.

Hybrid Organizations

Informal organizations are usually considered a hybrid because there is no identified leader, although an informal leader may emerge. When a leader does emerge, it is incumbent on this leader to foster solid relations with the employees in order to harness the energy of the informal organization to achieve greater productivity. Informal organizations tend to change over time, and they essentially follow the needs of the members associated with the organization. Leaders must be aware of changes as they take place. New informal leaders may emerge, and they too may become a source of actionable information. The business leader should be sensitive to the constantly changing social needs of the employees to ensure that the best level of productivity is obtained for the organization.

A second type of informal organization emerges to meet the needs of specific groups of employees who make up the organization. This is manifested in organizations in the form of informal clubs and off-work activities. For example, some organizations sponsor golf, bowling, or softball teams. These teams are composed of employees across several levels of the organization and tend to function as a hybrid organization within the framework of the formal structure.

A spiritual business organization creates an informal culture of inclusion to meet the specific needs of employees who make up the organization. Team building and forming strong relationships with coworkers are encouraged when the organization provides activities on company time. Employees participating in the spirited activities of the day develop a supportive environment. The organization provides employees with guided time for self-discovery as well as discovering special attributes of other employees. Special events are implemented to encourage spiritual growth and build interpersonal relationships. The results are that the employees will be more willing to help each other in a time of need.

Informal Organizations Within the Formal Structure

Informal structures operate within the formal structure, but leaders may emerge at any level. The military is an excellent example of informal organizations operating within a formal structure. The hierarchical structure is well established, but Navy chief petty officers, Army senior non-commissioned officers, and special operations groups from all services develop their own culture and their own forms of communication. These distinct suborganizations function in support of the formal organization but tend to get some tasks accomplished quicker and more effectively outside the formal structure. It is at this level that many changes are first observed and acted on in an informal manner.

Changes in Direction and Preference

Changes in direction, as communicated by the vision statement, and preference, as determined by the organizational culture, must be in alignment. In recent years, the public has become increasingly critical of behavior by corporate entities, as manifested by the actions of the leaders of the organizations. High-profile reports of misbehavior, moral turpitude, and violation of ethics among executives have resulted in the loss of market share and a loss of confidence by employees.[17] The Dynamic Strategies Model supports changes in direction from internal and external stimuli and changes in customer requirements, and it assists in mitigating the risks.

New Executives

New executives joining a spiritual business organization will need to be carefully mentored. The culture of the organization will quickly determine the suitability of the new executive. The custom of acceptance will work to assist in the acclimation of the new executive to the culture of the organization. Perhaps the biggest difference between most publically traded organizations and a spiritual business organization is the culture of ethical behavior that permeates the internal environment. When the new executive understands that ethical behavior is expected, assimilation into the organization begins. On assimilation into the organization, the new executive assists in the productivity by providing a moderating influence on job performance.[18] New executives are usually hired to lead a change effort and, if hired from outside the organization, will need to become familiar with the culture before they can be effective. Circumventing ethical behavior may become a temptation due to market pressures. As leaders become spiritualized, the culture of a spiritual business organization allows the application of the Dynamic Strategies Model to develop cost effectiveness by operating ethically.

Market Pressure Response

Responses to market pressures place great strains on leaders in an organization to act. Small business organizations must stay competitive in order to survive, and they should respond promptly to market demands as part of the survival process. Market-driven changes are often good because the pressure requires us to abandon the techniques that have outlived their usefulness in a highly competitive environment. The leader should be careful to distinguish between change for the sake of change and change for the benefit of the organization. Generally, the best guide to needed change is the customer.

Customer Needs

Customer demands are an excellent indicator of market conditions. The leader should be cautious to ensure that customer specifications are met or exceeded, with the approval of the customer. In addition, the leader must evaluate the trend in customer orders to determine the continued need for the deliverable, and should take early action to meet customer needs. Treating the customer as a stakeholder, and involving the customer in the strategic planning process, can assist greatly in ensuring that the needs of the customer will be met in the future. Some changes can be predicted. Customers create responses to change within their own organizations as well, and if the objectives can be matched, a partnership could develop to benefit both.

Acceptability of Risk and Uncertainty

Risk can usually be quantified in the process of developing a response to change. We usually see risk expressed in a dollar value or, less frequently, in terms of time and materials. There are many tools available to assess risk. What is missing are tools to assess uncertainty, which cannot be quantified. Uncertainty is developed based on the experience level of the leader in decision-making authority, and it often cannot be explained. Sometimes the risk may appear to be acceptable but will be deemed to be too uncertain by the leader and disapproved. At other times, the risk may seem to be high, but the leader will decide that the uncertainty factor is low enough to implement the change. These concepts are well covered in most management and leadership literature and are components of project management, so they will not be elaborated on further. The Dynamic Strategies Model accommodates risk and uncertainty by allowing decisions to be made at the most appropriate level.

Free Exchange of Information

The Dynamic Strategies Model is based on the free exchange of information across all levels of the organization. From the top down, the model requires the clear communication of direction in the form of the vision and mission statements. From leaders within the strategic business units, the goals are communicated across the organization and coordinated with other strategic business units as needed. The strategies to achieve the objectives, or tasks, can be generated at the most appropriate level. The appropriate level for determining the strategies to accomplish the tasks is at the level of performance. The Dynamic Strategies Model supports the free exchange of information in a culture that encourages employees to achieve their highest potential.

CHAPTER 12

Dynamic Implementations

Any model should be tested to determine the parameters of relevancy. The Dynamic Strategies Model may be scalable, but it has not been longitudinally tested in large organizations. The model has been developed over several years in theory and in practice, with the practice driving the changes to the model. The model, as it currently stands, does work in small organizations. The ability of the model to remain dynamic in larger organizations is unknown.

Examples

In this book, we have given real world examples of three small organizations. Each of these organizations has implemented the Dynamic Strategies Model. The small consulting firm was the foundation organization in which the model was implemented, tested, and initially modified. The single-person operation has been in business for more than 10 successful years. The owner now desires to retire but is having a difficult time trying to arrange for all of her customers to be adequately served after her retirement. The start-up consultancy is a new organization that is entering the market. In addition, several small business organizations in at least two countries with distinct cultures have implemented the model with success. Additional examples are not included because the evaluations of the other organizations was cross-sectional, while the small consulting firm and the single-person operation are longitudinal observations spanning more than ten years.

Small Consulting Firm

The vision statement of a small consulting firm providing project management and front-end logistics services was simply stated as, "Provide value to make the client successful." The rationale was that if the client was successful, the organization providing the services would also be successful.

The small consulting firm kept the mission statement very simple: "Work ourselves out of a job." This mission was intended to transfer sufficient knowledge to the client company so that they would no longer need to hire a consulting firm to accomplish the work. The rationale of the owner was that if every contract allowed an opportunity to assist the client company in being independent in the specific area in the future, the client would be delighted and, as a result, would recommend the consulting firm to others.

Single-Person Operation

The vision of the single owner-operator quilting business was informal and not recorded, but it was consistent over several years. The owner repeatedly stated that she was "doing what [was] fun and getting paid for it." The emphasis was on enjoying the hobby that had turned into a viable business and was quickly recognized as providing quality at a reasonable cost.

In the quilting business, there was no well-defined mission statement, but there was an operational definition that communicated added value to the customer. If necessary to articulate a mission statement, the single operator owner would return to statements such as, "Delivering good value" and "Providing the customer their money's worth."

Start-Up Consultancy

A current start-up consultancy consisting of a single owner identified the following vision statement, "Courage to become; strength to be more." The consultancy has a mission statement that supports the vision statement, while concentrating on day-to-day business operations, "Victory through every-day educational achievements." Dreams to become more than what we are are the key to future endeavors rising from the foundation of every-day achievements. Embracing dreams propels the individual forward and forms the future of our lives.

Template for Implementation

Implementing the Dynamic Strategies Model in your organization to develop a unique strategic plan that is brief, clear, and concise can follow a template. Although the content must reflect the desires of the owner or leader of the organization to place a personal mark on the direction the business is to follow, the process may be universal. The template provided here is a guide that can be easily modified to fit the needs of your organization. There is no single right way, only the way that works for you.

The name of organization should be at the top of the first page.

The vision statement should be brief, clear, concise, and understandable and should be center-justified immediately below the name of the organization. This statement should be no more than 25 to 50 words, with fewer words being best.

The mission statement should also be center-justified and placed immediately below the vision statement. The focus is on the small organization or the strategic business unit.

Goals can be manifold and may be listed on a separate page but should be brief, clear, concise, in consonance with the vision and mission statements and slightly "out of reach" to encourage motivation. This page of aggregate goals should be followed by each goal statement, with each one starting on a new page.

Objectives should be placed under the appropriate goal, using as many pages as is necessary. Each objective would then become a task statement presented at the top of the page and followed by the strategies that would be needed to accomplish the specific objective. It would help if the objective were stated in project management terms because so much of the objective translates directly to a task under that discipline. The metrics for the objective or task should also be included, along with guidance of when progress should be checked in a specific manner.

Strategies to achieve the objectives should consist of the time resources, prioritization, and placement of the objective in context. Start and end dates—and times, if applicable—should be included, along with any predecessors and successors that may be required by the nature of the objective being sought. Required resources should also be noted in as specific a manner as possible so that adequate planning can take place.

Summary

A strategic plan developed by applying the Dynamic Strategies Model remains robust, but it is still easy to understand and implement. More importantly, it is easy to modify the plan as needed and at the most appropriate level of the organization. As long as consonance with goals is maintained, the employee performing the work may modify the objective, and the strategy to achieve it, as needed to deliver the task on time, under budget, and to specification. The culture of the organization is at the foundation of the model, and the model lends itself to application in an organization of mutual trust and respect. Communication and transparency of intent allows employees to commit to the execution of the plan because the employee is involved in developing the strategies to attain the objectives. Leaders are removed from the need to micromanage daily activities, and cost savings result from a reduced level of oversight. When leaders are removed from the necessity to micromanage, they can devote more time to the global planning for which they are responsible. The Dynamic Strategies Model is effective in a secular setting, but it is more dynamic in a spiritual business organization headed by spiritualized leaders. The closer we come to achieving acceptance instead of tolerance, and the closer we come to mutual respect and trust across all levels of an organization, the closer we come to attaining greater productivity. When led by a spiritualized leader who cares about the employees, promotes organizational learning, empowers the employees, and promotes human potential, we begin to see a reduction in voluntary employee turnover, decreased litigation, higher levels of satisfaction, and increased profitability.

APPENDIX

A Template for Your Business

Name of Organization or Letterhead

—

Vision Statement

—

Mission Statement (Varies by SBU)

—

Goals (Created by executives within each SBU)

These goals are aggregated for the SBU and may include the person responsible for the goal.

Goal 1   Brief description, usually a few words, and slightly out of reach

Goal 2

Goal 3

Etc.

Goal 1

All objectives related to the goal are listed, usually by the task title. Sometimes a GANTT chart or network diagram may be included to visualize the timeline or relationships.

Objective 1a   Title of task

Objective 1b   Title of task

Objective 1c   Title of task

Etc.

Goal 2

Objective 2a

Objective 2b

Objective 2c

Etc.

Goal 3

Objective 3a

Objective 3b

Objective 3c

Etc.

Objective 1a

This is essentially the statement of work (SOW) and provides the detail necessary not only to perform the task but to measure the progress of the task. Sufficient information should be provided to allow those responsible for predecessor and successor tasks to understand how their performance affects the completion of the task on time, on budget, and to specification.

Restate Goal 1

Objective 1a Task Title

State the task briefly and clearly

Start date/time   **End date/time**

Predecessor task(s)

Successor task(s)

Timeline

Metrics

Checkpoints

Person responsible

Task sponsor or supervisor

Resources required

Objective 1b

Objective 1c

Notes

Introduction

1. There are many approaches to the preparation of strategic plans, and each has merit. The term "strategic plan" is used here in the generic sense and would generally apply to the linear approach of the planning process.
2. Bennis (1985).
3. Byars (1991).
4. Hill (1997).
5. Landrum & Gardner (2005).
6. Akella (2003).
7. Martin (2009).
8. U.S. Government, Small Business Administration, http://www.sba.gov/smallbusinessplanner/index.html

Chapter 1

1. Jensen (2005).
2. Seteroff (2003).
3. Campuzano (2010).
4. Mitroff & Denton (1999).
5. Seteroff (2003).

Chapter 2

1. Manyika, Roberts, & Sprague (2007).
2. The executive was a vice president of an engineering firm producing technical manuals for the U.S. Navy, and the initiative was to add a laminated card the same size as the company identification required to be worn at all times on site and at the customer location. The additional laminated card has the company vision statement on one side and the mission statement on the other.
3. U.S. Government, Small Business Administration, http://www.sba.gov/smallbusinessplanner/index.html
4. Hodgetts & Luthans (1994).
5. Richard Hodgetts, now deceased, made this statement in an address to a Nova Southeastern University doctoral seminar at the 1996 Academy of Management.

6. Marques (2006).

7. Campuzano (2010).

8. Knuutila (2003).

9. In 2003, Dr. Seteroff was called into a second-tier aerospace company in order to assist in determining a cost-effective procedure to systematically investigate manufacturing errors. After being unable to get to the root cause of the problem by interviewing the engineers responsible for the process and their supervisors, the author asked the mechanic operating the machine why there were so many rejects on the swing shift. The response was that he was able to reset the temperature boundaries, but the engineer in charge of that area of production on swing shift would not allow deviation from the process instructions. When asked why he did not raise this issue to his supervisor, his response was a classic, "Well, no one has ever asked me for my opinion before, and we are just not encouraged to say anything to the engineers."

10. Hodgetts & Luthans (1994).

11. Starkweather & Steinbacher (1998).

Chapter 3

1. Based on Pierce (1996) modified by Seteroff (1997, 2001. 2003, 2006, 2009); Seteroff & Campuzano (2009, 2010).

2. Kerzner (1998).

3. Breen (1995).

4. Hayden (2001).

5. Gray & Larson (2000).

6. Babu & Suresh (1996).

7. Seteroff (2009), "Introduction to Project Management" unpublished course presentation.

8. BrainyQuote (2010)

9. Vilalta-Perdo (2007).

10. Wheatley (1999).

11. Campuzano (2009).

12. Campbell (2007).

13. Campuzano (2009).

14. Seteroff (2003).

15. Campuzano (2009).

Chapter 4

1. Kerzner (2001).

2. Meredith & Mantel (2000).

3. Fabrycky & Blanchard (1991).

Chapter 5

1. General Electric, www.ge.com
2. "Change a light, Change the World," http://www.ge.com/products_services/lighting.html
3. General Electric, http://www.ge.com/products_services/aviation.html
4. The Coca-Cola Company, http://www.thecoca-colacompany.com/presscenter/nr_20091116_2020_vision.html
5. This company, Management & Logistics Associates, Inc., is no longer in business as an entity. On retirement of the owner, the several strategic business units were disposed of to employees of the organization.
6. Bandura (1977).
7. General Electric, www.ge.com
8. Iles & Yolles (2002).
9. Seteroff (2001).
10. Seteroff (2003).
11. Khadem (2008).
12. Management & Logistics Associates, Inc.

Chapter 6

1. The Coca-Cola Company (2010 para. 4) http://www.thecoca-colacompany.com/presscenter/nr_20091116_2020_vision.html
2. Edvinsson & Sullivan (1996).

Chapter 7

1. Avery, Hughes, Norman, & Luthans (2008).
2. Jurkiewicz & Giacalone (2004).
3. Jurkiewicz & Giacalone (2004).
4. Garcia-Zamor (2003, May/June).
5. Campuzano (2009).

Chapter 8

1. Aitkin (1995).
2. Maxwell (1998).

Chapter 9

1. Earley & Ang (2003).
2. Ng, Van Dyne, & Ang (2009).

3. Mahal (2009).

4. Egan (2008).

Chapter 10

1. Campuzano (2009).

2. Marques (2006).

3. Campuzano (2009).

4. Garcia-Zamor (2003, May/June).

5. Campuzano (2009).

6. Marques (2006).

7. Marques (2005, September).

8. Richard Hodgetts, now deceased, made this statement in an address to a Nova Southeastern University doctoral seminar at the 1996 Academy of Management.

9. Garcia-Zamor (2003, May/June).

10. Pittinsky (2009), p. 90.

11. Michelli (2007).

12. Levin & Gottlieb (2009).

13. Levin & Gottlieb (2009).

14. Morgan (2004).

Chapter 11

1. Source Watch: Corporate Social Responsibility.

2. Pittinsky (2009).

3. Wheatley (1999).

4. Chang & Wang (1995).

5. Campuzano (2009).

6. Starkweather & Steinbacher (1998).

7. Senge (1990a).

8. Senge (1990b).

9. Senge (1996).

10. Druskat & Wheeler (2003).

11. Argyris, Bellman, Blanchard, & Block (1994).

12. Campuzano & Seteroff (2010).

13. Wheatley (1999).

14. Cunliffe (2004).

15. Buchko (1994).

16. Baburajan (2008 November).

17. KPMG (2009); PricewaterhouseCoopers (2009).

18. Toor & Ofori (2009).

References

Aitkin, A. (1995). Vision only works if communicated. *Personnel Management, 1*(25), 28–29.

Akella, D. (2003). A question of power: How does management retain it? *Vikalpa: The Journal for Decision Makers, 28*(3), 45–56.

Argyris, C., Bellman, G. M., Blanchard, K., & Block, P. (1994). The future of workplace learning and performance. *Training & Development, 48*(5), S36–S47.

Avery, J. B., Hughes, L. W., Norman, S. M., & Luthans, K. W. (2008). Using positivity, transformational leadership and empowerment to combat employee negativity. *Leadership & Organization Development Journal, 29*, 110–126.

Baburajan, R. (2008 November) RingCentral Hosted Phone Services Reduce Overhead Costs for Small Businesses. Retrieved from http://www.tmcnet.com/channels/fax/articles/44673-ringcentral-hosted-phone-services-reduce-overhead-costs-small.htm

Bandura, A. (1977). *Self-efficacy: The exercise of control.* New York, NY: Freeman.

Babu, A. J. G., & Suresh, N. (1996). Project management with time, cost, and quality considerations. *European Journal of Operational Research, 88*(2), 320–327.

Bennis, W. (1985). *Leaders: Strategies for taking charge.* New York, NY: Harper Business.

BrainyQuote. (2010). Retrievedorm http://www.brainyquote.com/quotes/quotes/a/alanlakein154654.html

Breen, T. A. (1995). Project management: Developing the right "culture" can make a world of difference. *Plant Engineering, 49*(16), 110.

Buchko, A. A. (1994). Conceptualization and measurement of environmental uncertainty: An assessment of the miles and snow perceived environmental uncertainty scale. *Academy of Management Journal, 37*(2), 410–425.

Byars, L. L. (1991). *Strategic management: Formulation and implementation.* New York, NY: Harper Collins.

Campbell, C. R. (2007). On the journey toward wholeness in leader theories. *Leadership & Organization Development Journal, 28*(2), 137–153.

Campuzano, L. G. (2009). *A new leadership model to support spiritual organizational cultures after September 11, 2001.* Ann Arbor, MI: ProQuest LLC.

Campuzano, L. G., & Seteroff, S. S. (2010, February 15). A new approach to a spiritual business organization and employee satisfaction. *Social Science Research Network.*

Chang, C., & Wang, Y. (1995). A framework for understanding differences in labor turnover and human capital investment. *Journal of Economic Behavior & Organization, 28*(1), 91–105.

The Coca-Cola Company. *News Release* Retrieved from http://www.thecoca-colacompany.com/presscenter/nr_20091116_2020_vision.html

Cunliffe, A. L. (2004). On becoming a critically reflexive practitioner. *Journal of Management Education, 28*(4), 407.

Druskat, V. U., & Wheeler, J. V. (2003). Managing from the boundary: The effective leadership of self-managing work teams. *Academy of Management Journal, 46*(4), 435–457.

Earley, P. C., & Ang, S. (2003). *Cultural intelligence: Individual interactions across cultures.* Palo Alto, CA: Stanford University Press.

Edvinsson, L., & Sullivan, P. (1996). The epistemological challenge: Managing knowledge and intellectual capital. *European Management Journal 14*(4), 356–364.

Egan, T. M. (2008). The relevance of organizational subculture for motivation to transfer learning. *Human Resource Development Quarterly, 19*(4), 299–322.

Fabrycky, W. J., & Blanchard, B. S. (1991). *Life-cycle cost and economic analysis.* Englewood Cliffs, NJ: Prentice-Hall.

Garcia-Zamor, J. (2003, May/June). Workplace spirituality and organizational performance. *Public Administration Review, 63*(3) 355–363.

General Electric Company. *Change a light, Change the World.* Retrieved from http://www.ge.com/products_services/lighting.html

General Electric Company. *GE Imagination at Work.* Retrieved from http://www.ge.com

Gray, C. F., & Larson, E. W. (2000). *Project management: The managerial process.* Boston, MA: Irwin McGraw-Hill.

Hayden, W. M. (2001). The emerging role of project management. *Leadership & Management in Engineering, 1*(2), 48.

Hill, C. W. L. (1997). Establishing a standard: Competitive strategy and technological standards in winner-take-all industries. *Academy of Management Executive, 11*(2), 7–25.

Hodgetts, R. M., & Luthans, F. (1994). New paradigm organizations: From total quality to learning to world-class. *Organizational Dynamics, 22*(3), 4.

Iles, P., & Yolles, M. (2002). Across the great divide: HRD, technology translation, and knowledge migration in bridging the knowledge gap between SMEs and universities. *Human Resource Development International, 5*(1), 23–53.

Jensen, M. C. (2005). Modern industrial revolution, exit, and the failure of internal control systems (May 9, 1999 ed.) Harvard Business School, *Social Science Electronic Publishing.*

Jurkiewicz, C. L., & Giacalone, R. A. (2004). A values framework for measuring the impact of workplace spirituality on organizational performance. *Ethics* *49*(2) 129.

Kerzner, H. (1998). *In search of excellence in project management: Successful practices in high performance organizations.* New York, NY: Van Nostrand Reinhold.

Kerzner, H. (2001). *Project management.* New York, NY: Wiley.

Khadem, R. (2008). Alignment and follow-up: Steps to strategy execution. *Journal of Business Strategy, 29*(6) 29-35.

Knuutila, E. (2003). *First mover advantage: Under what kind of conditions does it have the most effect?* China Economic Network. Peking University Education Foundation, Beijing, China

KPMG. (2009, August 25). KPMG's *Fraud Survey 2009.* Retrieved from http://www.kpmg.com/aci/docs/insights/21001NSS_Fraud_Survey_082409.pdf

Landrum, N. E., & Gardner, C. L. (2005). Using integral theory to effect strategic change. *Journal of Organizational Change Management, 18*(3), 247.

Levin, I., & Gottlieb, J. Z. (2009) Realigning organization culture for optimum performance: Six principles and eight practices. *Organization Development Journal, 27*(4), 31.

Mahal, P. K. (2009). Organizational culture and organizational climate as a determinant of motivation. *The ICFAI Journal of Management Research, 8*(10), 38–52.

Manyika, J. M., Roberts, R. P., & Sprague, K. L. (2007, December). Information technology: Eight business technology trends to watch. *The McKinsey Quarterly*, p. 10.

Marques, J. (2005, September). Yearning for a more spiritual workplace. *Journal of American Academy of Business, Cambridge, 7*, 149–152.

Marques, J. (2006). The spiritual worker: An examination of the ripple effect that enhances quality of life in - and outside the work environment. *The Journal of Management Development, 25*(9), 884–895.

Martin, S. (2009). *Small business employment.* Retrieved April 28, 2009, from http://www.askjim.biz/answers/small-business-employment_517.php

Maxwell, J. C. (1998). *The 21 irrefutable laws of leadership: Follow them and people will follow you.* Nashville, TN: Thomas Nelson Publishers.

Meredith, J. R., & Mantel, S. J. (2000). *Project management: A managerial approach.* New York, NY: Wiley.

Michelli, J. A. (2007). *The Starbucks experience: Five principles for turning ordinary into extraordinary.* New York, NY: McGraw-Hill.

Mitroff, I. I., & Denton, E. A. (1999). *A spiritual audit of corporate America.* San Francisco, CA: Jossey-Bass.

Morgan, J. F. (2004). How should business respond to a more religious workplace? *S.A.M. Advanced Management Journal, 69*(4), 11–19.

Ng, K. Y., Van Dyne, L., & Ang, S. (2009). From experience to experiential learning: Cultural intelligence as a learning capability for global leader development. *Academy of Management Learning & Education, 8*(4) 511–526.

Pittinsky, T. L. (2009). *Crossing the divide: Intergroup leadership in a world of difference.* Boston, MA: Harvard Business Press.

PricewaterhouseCoopers. (2009). *Fraud in a downturn: A review of how fraud and other integrity risks affect business.* Retrieved from http://www.pwc.com/en_US/us/forensic-services/assets/fraud-downturn.pdf

Senge, P. M. (1990a). *The fifth discipline: The art and practice of the learning organization.* San Francisco, CA: Berrett Koehler.

Senge, P. M. (1990b). The leader's new work: Building learning organizations. *Sloan Management Review, 32*(1), 8.

Senge, P. M. (1996). Leading learning organizations. *Executive Excellence, 13*(4), 10.

Seteroff, S. S. (2001). *Return of the generalist: Managers in a trans-disciplinary environment. International Logistics Conference.* Paper presented at the conference of the SOLE The International Society for Logistics, Orlando, FL.

Seteroff, S. S. (2003). *Beyond leadership to followership.* Victoria, BC: Trafford.

Source Watch: *Corporate Social Responsibility.* Retrieved from http://www.sourcewatch.org/index.php?title=Corporate_Social_Responsibility

Starkweather, R. A., & Steinbacher, C. L. (1998). Job satisfaction affects the bottom line. *HR Magazine, 43*(10), 110–112.

Toor, S. R., & Ofori, G. (2009). Ethical leadership: Examining the relationships with full range leadership model, employee outcomes, and organizational culture. *Journal of Business Ethics, 90*(4), 533–547.

US Government, Small Business Administration. Retrieved from http://www.sba.gov/

Vilalta-Perdo, W. (2007). Information systems project management: Methods, tools and techniques. *Interfaces, 37*(4), 392–394.

Wheatley, M. J. (1999). *Lessons from the new workplace.* [Motion picture] USA: CRM Films, L.P.

Index

Note: The *italicized f* following page numbers refers to figures.